When AI Goes Wrong:

Lessons from Real-World Failures

By Anthony Altamura

Copyright and Disclaimer

First Edition
Self-Published

The information provided in this book is for educational and informational purposes only. While every effort has been made to ensure the accuracy of the content, the author and publisher make no representations or warranties of any kind regarding the completeness, accuracy, or suitability of this information for any purpose. The author and publisher shall not be held liable for any loss, financial or otherwise, resulting from the use of this book.

Readers are encouraged to seek professional advice before implementing any suggestions or making business decisions based on the material in this book.

When AI Goes Wrong: Lessons from Real-World Failures

Table of Contents

Author Bio

Dr. Anthony Altamura is a highly regarded expert in predictive analytics, risk management, and management consulting, with over 20 years of experience across multiple industries. He began his career in the fast-moving consumer goods (FMCG) sector, where he applied advanced analytics to sales forecasting, optimizing business performance and inventory management through data-driven strategies.

Building on this, he transitioned to the banking industry, where he led high-performing analytics teams at a major international bank. In this role, he was responsible for predictive credit analytics and risk management, overseeing the development and implementation of models that improved risk and financial forecasting and enhanced risk assessment frameworks. This included building early credit alert models utilizing machine learning techniques. Under his leadership, the bank significantly advanced its analytical capabilities to drive operational efficiency and modernize decision-making processes in a highly competitive sector.

He later founded his own consulting firm, where he has successfully advised top-tier financial institutions and FinTech companies. His work includes:

- Automating credit origination processes.
- Advising on best practice model validation techniques and frameworks.
- Building credit and liquidity stress testing models and platforms.
- Developing customized business applications and tools for clients.
- Providing risk management advisory.
- Offering business consulting and coaching.

His expertise in business and predictive analytics has made him a trusted advisor in helping businesses modernize their risk management practices and leverage AI for enhanced decision-making.

Dr. Altamura holds a PhD in Finance, with a research focus on predicting financial distress of listed companies. Throughout his academic work and professional experience, he has applied advanced statistical and machine learning techniques such as logistic regression, decision trees, neural networks, ensemble models, and support vector machines. His ability to bridge cutting-edge approaches with practical business solutions has made him a sought-after leader in the field.

His book, *When AI Goes Wrong: Lessons from Real-World Failures,* offers a deep dive into the critical lessons learned from AI missteps across various industries. Drawing on decades of hands-on experience, Dr. Altamura equips business leaders with actionable insights on how to avoid common pitfalls and leverage AI responsibly. By focusing on real-world examples of AI failures, he provides practical strategies for integrating AI into business operations while prioritizing ethical standards, transparency, and resilience in the face of rapid technological change.

Introduction: The Promise and Perils of AI

In today's fast-paced digital era, artificial intelligence (AI) is reshaping industries on an unprecedented scale. From revolutionizing business operations to driving breakthroughs in healthcare, AI's potential to create new opportunities and unlock immense value seems limitless. It's a game changer, pushing the boundaries of what technology can achieve. However, with great power comes great responsibility and significant risk. For every success story showcasing AI's transformative impact, there's a cautionary tale underscoring the dangers of deploying this technology without rigorous oversight. When AI systems fail, the consequences can be far-reaching, exposing vulnerabilities and creating new challenges that we are only beginning to understand.

The Bright Side of AI: Transformative Success Stories

AI's promise has been realized in several industries, driving significant advances. Take Netflix, for example, which uses AI to power more than 80% of its viewer recommendations (Lighthouse Labs, 2020). By analyzing user behavior through machine learning algorithms, Netflix offers personalized content that boosts engagement and increases viewer retention, ultimately driving revenue growth.

In agriculture, AI is making strides through innovations like John Deere's See & Spray Ultimate technology. Using advanced machine learning and computer vision, this system helps farmers precisely target weeds with herbicides, reducing chemical usage by up to 66% and promoting more sustainable farming practices (Future Farming, 2023).

Retail is another sector benefiting from AI's capabilities. Starbucks has harnessed AI for personalized marketing, using customer data like past purchases and even weather patterns to deliver tailored recommendations through its mobile app. On hot days, for example, customers receive offers for cold beverages, while personalized rewards are sent based on individual buying habits. This AI-driven personalization has significantly increased customer engagement and sales (Harvard Business Review, 2023).

These examples showcase AI's ability to drive efficiency, accuracy, and innovation across industries. However, as much as AI enhances operations and transforms businesses, it is not without flaws. When not properly designed, tested, or implemented, AI systems can fail, and the consequences can be severe.

The Dark Side of AI: Failures with Consequences

While AI offers boundless opportunities, its failures remind us of the technology's limitations. One of the most high-profile cases involved Uber's self-driving car, which tragically struck and killed a pedestrian during a test. The AI system failed to detect the pedestrian correctly, highlighting critical gaps in safety protocols. This incident serves as a stark warning about the dangers of deploying AI without rigorous safeguards (The Verge, 2018).

In the world of finance, Zillow's home-buying algorithm is another cautionary tale. Designed to estimate home values and make purchasing decisions, the algorithm faltered in an unpredictable housing market, leading to the failure of the "Zillow Offers" program. The resulting financial losses were immense, exposing the limitations of AI in fast-changing, dynamic markets where human judgment is crucial (Stanford Graduate School of Business, 2021).

Similarly, the Boeing 737 Max crashes underscored the dangers of over-reliance on automated systems. The aircraft's automated system, meant to prevent stalling, malfunctioned due to faulty sensor data, and the lack of pilot control options exacerbated the situation. This tragedy revealed the need for human intervention in high-stakes environments like aviation (RSNA, 2020; News.com.au, 2020).

Facial recognition technology has also faced significant setbacks. Amazon's Rekognition software incorrectly matched 28 U.S. Congress members with criminal mugshots, and a disproportionate number of those misidentified were black congress members. This sparked concerns about the fairness and accuracy of deploying facial recognition in law enforcement, where errors can have serious ethical and operational implications (BBC, 2018).

These cases highlight the risks of AI when it fails. Whether the consequences are financial, reputational, or human, the message is clear: while AI is powerful, it must be developed and implemented with thorough testing, transparency, and human oversight to avoid catastrophic outcomes.

The Need for Responsible AI Development

The key to harnessing AI's potential while mitigating its risks lies in responsible development, implementation, and governance. AI is not a magic solution, it is a tool that requires ongoing oversight, ethical considerations, and a continuous feedback loop to ensure it remains reliable, accurate, and fair. Systems need to be designed with transparency, rigorously tested with diverse datasets, and continuously monitored to guarantee they function as intended.

When AI is implemented responsibly, it can unlock extraordinary value. But without proper checks and balances, it can result in unintended consequences—from biased algorithms to systems that override human decision-making. These risks must be carefully managed to prevent AI failures that erode trust and cause harm.

What to Expect in This Book

This book delves deep into AI failures, exploring real-life case studies that demonstrate where things went wrong and why. More importantly, it uncovers the lessons these failures offer for future AI development. Through a focus on areas like data quality, algorithmic bias, human oversight, and ethical design, this book provides insights into how businesses and developers can implement AI in safer, more ethical ways.

Each chapter focuses on a specific aspect of AI failure, from healthcare to finance, transportation, and beyond. By studying these failures, readers will be equipped to build more resilient, ethical, and successful AI systems.

Chapter 1: Historical AI Incidents

As artificial intelligence (AI) continues to revolutionize industries and become a ubiquitous part of everyday life, the risks associated with its rapid deployment are becoming increasingly evident. The proliferation of AI-powered technologies across sectors ranging from healthcare to finance and transportation has introduced new vulnerabilities, with systems occasionally failing or even causing harm. These AI incidents expose the complexity and unpredictability of deploying AI on a large scale, particularly in environments where human lives, finances, and reputations are at stake.

In recent years, the surge in AI product development has only amplified these risks. The competitive pressure to innovate and release new AI systems has led to a flood of AI-powered tools and applications hitting the market, many of which are often under-tested and rushed into production. This race to capitalize on AI's transformative potential has created an environment where incidents are becoming more frequent, as developers and companies prioritize speed over thorough risk management and safety protocols.

From self-driving cars to financial algorithms, AI systems are being integrated into high-stakes areas of society, where even minor failures can have serious consequences. These incidents are not confined to niche sectors but occur across a vast range of industries, illustrating the broad impact of AI on modern life. To fully appreciate the importance and implications of these incidents, we must first clarify what we mean by **AI**, **AI systems**, and **AI incidents**.

Defining AI and AI Systems

For the purposes of this book, **artificial intelligence (AI)** refers to the capability of machines to perform functions typically thought of as requiring human intelligence, such as reasoning, recognizing patterns or understanding natural language. AI includes, but is not limited to, machine learning – a set of techniques by which a computer system learns how to perform a task through recognizing patterns in data and inferring decision rules (AI Incident Database, 2024).

An **AI system** is any technology or process in which AI plays a meaningful role, though it may include components that do not involve AI, such as mechanical parts. Examples of AI systems include self-driving cars, facial-recognition software, Google Translate, and credit-scoring algorithms. In some cases, even non-AI algorithms can be considered part of an AI system when human decision-making authority is transferred to the system. For example, a hospital system selects vaccine candidates based on a series of hand tailored rules in a black box algorithm (AI Incident Database, 2024).

What is an AI Incident?

An **AI incident** is defined as an alleged harm or near harm event to people, property, or the environment where an AI system is implicated (AI Incident Database, 2024). These incidents can arise from technical errors, bias in data, or failures in the interaction between humans and AI systems. They can result in financial losses, reputational damage, discrimination, or even physical harm, depending on the sector and application.

Take, for example, a self-driving car that misinterprets a traffic situation, leading to a crash, or a facial-recognition system that incorrectly identifies someone, resulting in a wrongful arrest. In both cases, the AI system didn't function as intended, and real-world harm followed.

The Competitive Rush for AI Products

Understanding AI incidents is crucial, especially as AI technologies continue to evolve rapidly. The competitive landscape for AI has intensified, with companies racing to release new AI products to stay ahead of rivals. This became particularly evident following the release of **ChatGPT in 2022**, which sparked accelerated AI development across industries. Large tech companies, startups, and even smaller developers have been under immense pressure to launch AI products quickly, often sacrificing thorough testing and consideration of potential risks.

While competition drives innovation, it also introduces risks. Companies may release AI systems that are underdeveloped, insufficiently tested, or based on biased data, contributing to the rise in AI incidents. As these AI systems are pushed to market before, they are ready for real-world deployment, they may malfunction, make flawed decisions, or fail to meet ethical and safety standards, leading to unintended harm.

Trends in AI Incidents

The **AI Incident Database** (AIID) tracks and documents AI-related failures across industries (McGregor, 2021). One of the key takeaways from this database is the increasing number of reported incidents over the years, as AI systems become more widespread and embedded in critical areas of society. As of September 2024 the **AI Incident Database** had 795 incidents reported, spanning from 1983 to current. The incidents in the database demonstrate that AI failures are not confined to niche technologies but are present across various fields and span across many different applications.

AI Incidents Over Time

Since 2019, there has been a steady rise in the number of reported AI incidents. This growth reflects both the expanding use of AI systems and increased awareness of the potential risks. The data shows that as AI technologies become more complex, the likelihood of errors or unintended consequences also increases. From early challenges in facial recognition accuracy to more recent problems with autonomous vehicles and deep fakes, these incidents highlight the evolving nature of AI risks.

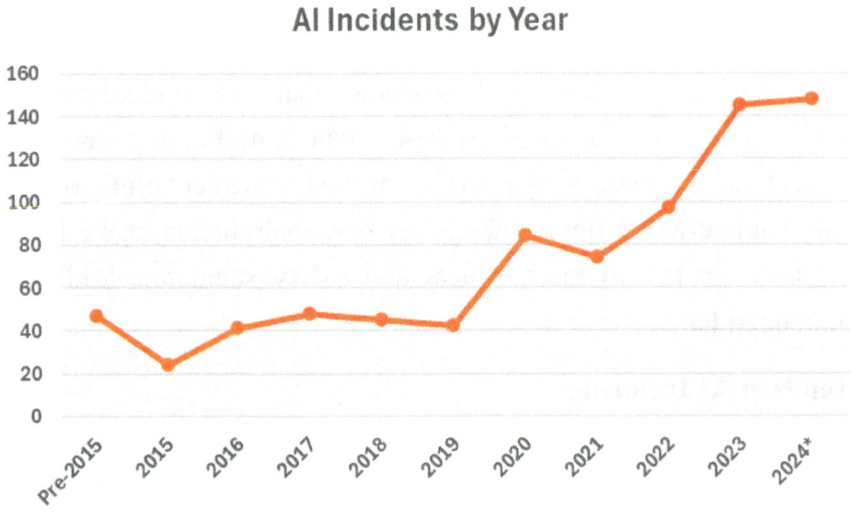

2024 incidents are only captured up until September.

From early missteps in facial recognition to recent challenges with autonomous vehicles and deep fakes, these incidents reveal the growing complexity and risks associated with AI. As shown in the chart above, as of September 2024, there have already been 148 incidents reported. As AI becomes more prevalent and companies continue to rapidly compete in releasing AI products, it is expected that this number will continue to rise at pace.

These AI incidents are not limited to small startups or inexperienced developers. The AI Incident Database includes reports from a broad range of developer types, including large tech companies, academic institutions, government entities, and startups. The top five developers with the highest incidents on the database are Facebook/Meta, Tesla, Google, OpenAi and Amazon. Whether the AI system is developed by a global corporation or a smaller team, the challenges remain consistent: ensuring that the system works as intended in real-world conditions, free from bias, and transparent in its decision-making processes.

AI Incidents Causing Harm by Industry and Harm Distribution Bias

Understanding where AI causes harm is crucial for assessing its impact and ensuring responsible development. The Center for Security and Emerging Technology (CSET) AI Harm Taxonomy for AIID is a framework that classifies AI-related incidents based on the harms, entities involved, technologies used, and the context in which they occur.

To qualify as AI harm, the following four elements must be present:

1. An **entity** that experienced
2. a **harm event** or **harm issue** that
3. can be **directly linked** to a consequence of the behavior of
4. an **AI system**.

Only incidents with all four elements are considered AI harm. Not every incident in AIID meets this definition of AI harm. The incidents that have met the AI harm criteria have been segmented by sector and harm distribution bias. The data for all charts in this chapter is sourced from the **AI Incident Database** (McGregor, 2021).

As shown in the chart below AI incidents causing harm, have been recorded across multiple sectors, including Information and communication, healthcare, finance, transportation, and law enforcement. Each of these sectors presents unique challenges when it comes to deploying AI systems. In healthcare, for instance, AI tools are used to assist in diagnosis and treatment recommendations, and errors in these systems can lead to critical medical decisions being compromised. In law enforcement, the use of AI for facial recognition has led to significant concerns about racial bias and wrongful identification.

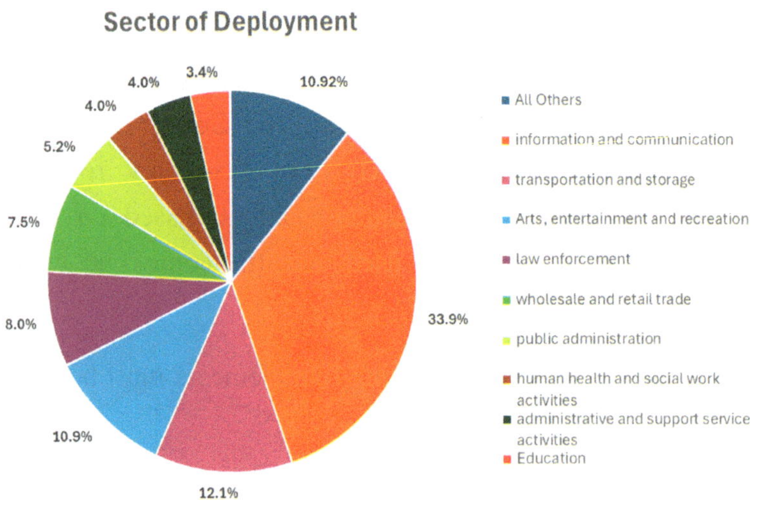

In addition to industry-specific incidents, it's important to understand harm distribution bias in AI systems. As shown in the Harm Distribution Bias chart, a significant portion of identified biases involve attributes such as race, sex, and religion, with race being the most commonly cited, followed by sex and religion. These biases can lead to disproportionate harm to specific groups, perpetuating existing inequalities and introducing new risks.

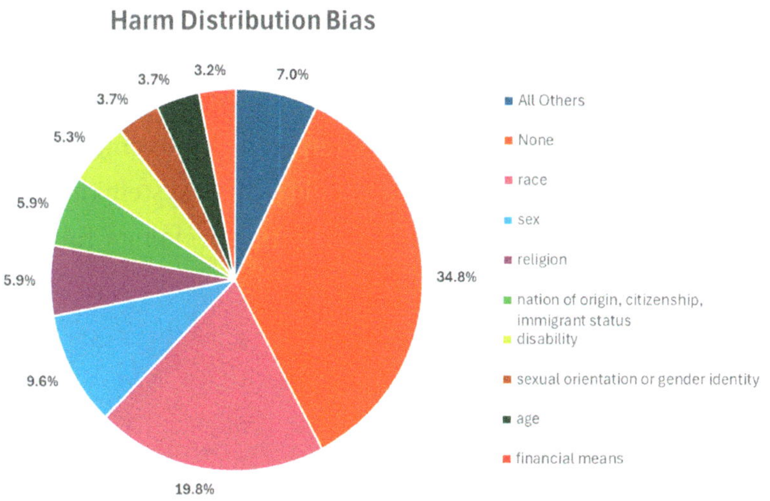

Understanding and addressing these biases is crucial for ensuring fairness and equity in AI applications. By identifying where these biases occur, developers and policymakers can take targeted action to mitigate harm and improve the design of AI systems, ultimately fostering more ethical and responsible AI use across industries.

AI Incident Goal, Technology Used and Technical Failure Reason

The AIID has a breakdown of AI incidents by the **Goals, Methods, and Failures (GMF) Taxonomy,** which is a framework designed to categorize AI-related incidents by focusing on three key aspects:

1. **Goals**: The real-world tasks or objectives the AI system is intended to perform, such as facial recognition or decision-making.
2. **Methods**: The specific technologies and techniques used to implement the AI system, such as machine learning models (e.g., Transformers) or other algorithms.
3. **Failures**: The technical reasons behind system failures that result in harm, such as concept drift or data errors.

This framework is valuable because it helps developers and researchers link failures to specific goals and methods, providing a clearer understanding of the root causes of AI-related harm. By identifying these failures, the taxonomy enables targeted improvements, reducing risks and enhancing the safety and reliability of AI systems in real-world applications. Below are three charts reporting incidents following the GMF taxonomy:

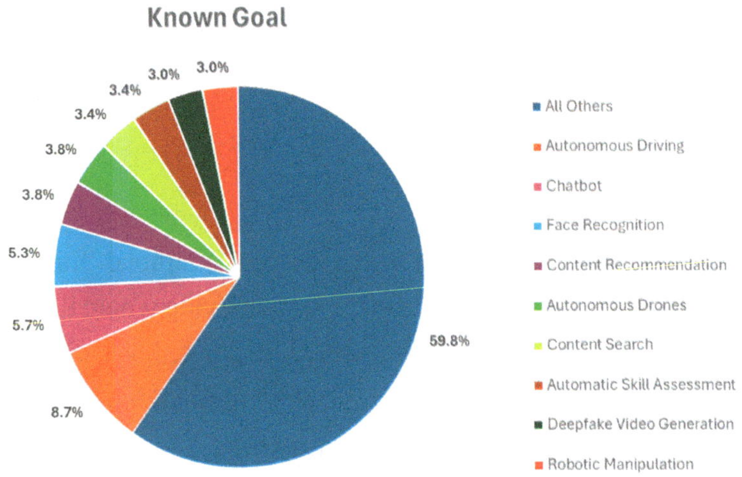

The chart on AI goals above shows that 60% of incidents involve a wide range of goals categorized as "all others," with the top three specific goals being autonomous driving, chatbots, and facial recognition. This distribution highlights the significant diversity in AI applications, reflecting the vast potential AI holds across industries. It is crucial to understand the range of goals because each goal presents unique risks and challenges. For instance, the complexity of autonomous driving systems differs significantly from that of chatbots. Tracking these metrics can help developers and stakeholders anticipate where AI incidents are most likely to occur and prepare mitigation strategies accordingly.

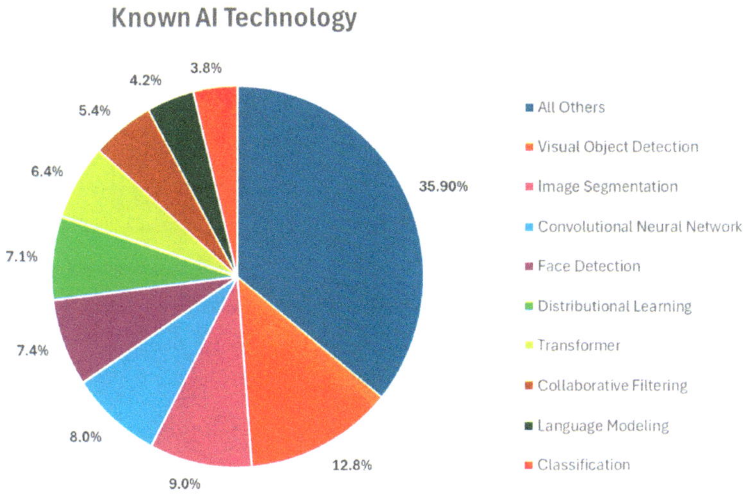

The chart above reveals that one-third of AI incidents involve a variety of less common technologies, while the top three technologies most frequently implicated in incidents are visual object detection, image segmentation, and convolutional neural networks (CNNs). Understanding which technologies are associated with the most incidents is crucial for improving AI system robustness. Visual object detection and image segmentation are key components in applications like autonomous vehicles and medical diagnostics, where errors can have serious consequences. Similarly, convolutional neural networks are widely used in pattern recognition tasks, making them central to many AI systems but also vulnerable to failures when not properly trained or tested. Monitoring the percentage of incidents linked to each technology and their performance in real-world scenarios helps identify where these systems are most likely to encounter technical challenges and where improvements are needed.

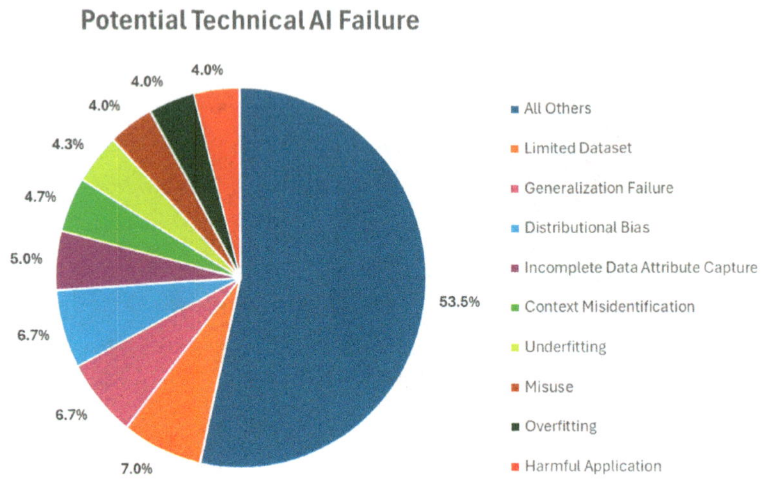

The chart on potential technical failures shows that about half of the incidents arise from a diverse set of categorized issues, with the top three specific failures being limited datasets, generalization failure, and distribution bias. These failures are critical to understand because they reflect fundamental weaknesses in the AI development process. Limited datasets hinder a system's ability to learn and generalize, while generalization failure prevents AI from functioning effectively in new or diverse situations. Distribution bias, where AI systems struggle to perform accurately across different demographic or data distributions, presents both ethical and operational risks. Other significant issues include incomplete data and overfitting or underfitting, which further emphasize the importance of data quality and model performance in ensuring reliable AI systems. Monitoring the prevalence of each failure type, as well as improvements in AI training methodologies, is essential for enhancing the reliability and fairness of AI systems in the future.

Conclusion: Why This Data Matters

The data and trends outlined in this chapter are crucial because they illustrate the broad and multifaceted nature of AI incidents, serving as a foundation for the deeper analysis to follow. As shown by the data, AI incidents are not confined to a single industry or goal but occur across a wide range of sectors, technologies, and objectives from healthcare to finance, and from autonomous driving to facial recognition. Moreover, the incidents arise from a variety of technical failures, such as limited datasets, generalization failure, and distribution bias, each posing significant challenges.

This diverse set of incidents highlights that AI systems can fail for many reasons, whether due to the technology itself, ethical considerations, or operational weaknesses. These failures can lead to significant harm, affecting individuals, businesses, and entire industries. As highlighted throughout the chapter, incidents in sectors like healthcare and law enforcement demonstrate the potential for severe consequences, from compromised medical decisions to wrongful identification. By understanding the patterns and causes of these incidents, we gain valuable insights into the inherent risks associated with AI deployment, allowing us to identify necessary steps to mitigate these risks in future AI development.

The data also shows that AI failures are not isolated to specific technologies or developers; they are present across a range of systems and entities, from major tech companies to smaller developers. This underlines the importance of addressing AI risks holistically, considering both technical improvements and the broader ethical and regulatory landscape. Developers, businesses, and policymakers must all play a role in addressing the risks outlined, ensuring that AI systems are robust, fair, and safe for widespread deployment.

In the following chapters, we will build on this data, exploring specific cases of AI failure to better understand how we can create safer, more reliable, and ethical AI systems. This exploration will emphasize that as AI systems grow more widespread, so too must our efforts to manage and mitigate their risks.

Looking Ahead: Key Reasons Why AI Fails

In this chapter, we have seen that AI incidents can occur across various sectors, highlighting the diversity of failures from self-driving cars to facial recognition systems. But what causes these AI systems to fail? In the next chapter, we will dive deeper into the **key reasons why AI fails**. From poor data quality and algorithmic bias to overfitting and technical malfunctions, we will explore the root causes that lead to AI failures. Understanding these causes is essential for building more robust, fair, and reliable AI systems, helping to prevent the incidents we discussed in this chapter from recurring.

Chapter 2: Key Reasons Why AI Fails

Artificial Intelligence (AI) has become an integral part of many industries, driving innovation and offering unprecedented efficiency. From automating routine tasks to enabling complex decision-making processes, AI's capabilities are transforming sectors such as healthcare, finance, transportation, and more. However, alongside its promise, AI has also demonstrated its potential for failure in ways that can lead to serious financial losses, ethical dilemmas, and even harm to individuals or society. Understanding why AI fails is crucial for those who develop, implement, or interact with these systems.

AI failures can arise from various causes poor data, algorithmic bias, technical issues, or ethical oversights and often result from a combination of these factors. While AI systems can learn and adapt, they are not immune to the limitations and biases that come from the data and models they are built upon. Additionally, the rapid development of AI technology has outpaced the establishment of regulatory frameworks, leaving gaps in oversight and accountability.

The purpose of this chapter is to provide a broad overview of **fifteen key reasons** why AI fails. By exploring these failure mechanisms, we gain insight into the complex, interconnected challenges that must be addressed to prevent future failures. Although the case studies discussed in later chapters will delve into specific examples, this chapter serves as a foundation for understanding the broader reasons behind AI failures and their implications.

1. Data Quality Issues

AI systems are highly dependent on the data on which they are trained. When the data is flawed whether due to incompleteness, bias, or inaccuracies the AI's outputs will be similarly flawed. This problem is often summarized by the phrase "garbage in, garbage out." AI models cannot function effectively if their foundational data is poor.

Common data quality problems include insufficient diversity in the training data, historical biases, or outdated information. If the data does not represent the full range of situations the AI will encounter in the real world, the system's predictions or decisions will be unreliable.

- **Example**: An AI-based healthcare diagnostic tool trained on incomplete patient data failed to diagnose illnesses accurately, leading to incorrect treatments being recommended.

2. Algorithmic Bias

AI systems are not inherently neutral. They learn from the data they are given, which often reflects the biases present in society. As a result, AI can reproduce and even exacerbate these biases, leading to unfair or discriminatory outcomes.

Bias in AI can affect critical decisions, particularly in areas like hiring, law enforcement, or lending. If the training data reflects historical inequalities, the AI will likely perpetuate these biases, disproportionately affecting certain groups. Ensuring that AI systems are fair and unbiased requires carefully auditing and adjusting both the data and the algorithms.

- **Example**: An AI-driven hiring system prioritized candidates based on past hiring data that favored a specific demographic, leading to an unfair exclusion of candidates from underrepresented groups.

3. Overfitting and Underfitting

When training an AI model, there is a delicate balance between **overfitting** and **underfitting**. Overfitting occurs when a model is too closely aligned with its training data, learning irrelevant patterns or noise that don't generalize well to new data. Underfitting happens when the model is too simplistic and fails to capture important trends in the data, leading to poor performance both during training and in real-world applications.

Overfitting can result in an AI system that performs well in controlled environments but fails when confronted with new, real-world situations. Underfitting, on the other hand, results in a system that underperforms overall and fails to meet basic expectations.

- **Example**: An AI-based customer service chatbot overfitted to specific, scripted conversations during its training, but struggled to handle real-world interactions with diverse customer queries.

4. Over-Reliance on Historical Data

AI systems often depend on historical data to make future predictions. However, when these models over-rely on static, outdated information, they can fail to adapt to new conditions. Over-reliance on historical data makes AI models less responsive to changing trends or dynamic environments, leading to inaccurate predictions or recommendations.

For AI systems to remain relevant and effective, they must be regularly updated with current data and recalibrated to reflect changing circumstances. Models based solely on historical data are likely to fail when conditions shift.

- **Example**: An AI-based stock-trading system that wasn't updated to account for new market conditions ended up making incorrect predictions, leading to significant financial losses for firms that relied too heavily on outdated models.

5. Lack of Explainability (The Black Box Problem)

Many AI systems, particularly those built on deep learning, operate as "black boxes." This means that even the developers may not fully understand how the AI is making its decisions. When AI systems are opaque, it becomes difficult to trust their outputs or to address mistakes when they occur.

Explainability is crucial in high-stakes environments like healthcare, finance, and criminal justice, where decisions can have serious consequences. If an AI system cannot provide a clear, understandable explanation of how it arrived at a decision, it becomes impossible to scrutinize or challenge its outputs, which undermines trust and accountability.

- **Example**: A financial institution relied on an AI system to assess loan applications, but when certain approvals led to defaults, the system's decision-making process could not be explained or understood by the team responsible for reviewing the loans.

6. Lack of Human Oversight

Even the most advanced AI systems require human oversight to function properly and ethically. Over-relying on AI without human intervention can lead to critical errors, as AI struggles with the complexities and unpredictability of real-world situations. AI can process data and make decisions quickly, but it lacks the human ability to interpret context, values, and ethical nuances.

Human oversight is especially crucial in sectors like healthcare, transportation, and law enforcement, where mistakes can have severe consequences. AI should support human decision-making, not replace it entirely. In high-risk environments, human intervention is necessary to ensure AI systems remain accountable and aligned with ethical standards.

- **Example**: An autonomous vehicle's AI system failed to correctly identify a pedestrian crossing the street, leading to a preventable accident. Human oversight could have averted this tragic outcome.

7. Lack of Real-World Testing (Sim-to-Real Gap)

AI systems that perform well in controlled environments or simulations often fail when deployed in real-world settings due to the **sim-to-real gap**. Controlled environments can never fully replicate the complexities and unpredictability of real-world conditions. When AI models aren't tested in diverse and dynamic environments, they risk failure once they leave the lab.

- **Example**: An AI system designed to manage urban traffic flow performed well in simulations but struggled to adapt to real-world traffic conditions, which involved unpredictable human behavior and varying road conditions.

8. Lack of Continuous Monitoring and Updating

AI models must evolve to stay relevant. Without continuous monitoring, regular updates, and a feedback loop between the system and real-world outcomes, AI systems can become outdated and less effective over time. As real-world conditions change, models trained on static datasets require constant recalibration to maintain their accuracy and adapt to new patterns or data. A well-designed feedback loop helps AI systems learn from their environment and correct errors, ensuring they remain responsive to changing conditions.

- **Example**: An AI model used for predictive maintenance in industrial equipment failed to account for evolving operational conditions. Without a feedback loop and continuous updates, the system's predictions became less accurate over time, leading to unexpected equipment failures.

9. Technical Failures

Despite the sophistication of AI systems, they are still susceptible to technical errors such as bugs, glitches, or hardware malfunctions. Technical failures can lead to unexpected behavior, financial loss, or even safety risks. While some technical issues can be anticipated, others may emerge only after the AI system is deployed in a real-world setting.

The complexity of AI systems makes them particularly vulnerable to technical failures, especially in cases where the technology is deployed without sufficient testing or monitoring. Robust technical safeguards are essential to minimize the impact of these failures.

- **Example**: An AI-driven logistics system experienced a technical malfunction, resulting in delays and mismanagement of inventory, causing widespread operational disruptions.

10. Poor Integration with Existing Systems

AI rarely operates in isolation. For AI to deliver its full value, it must integrate smoothly with existing technologies, processes, and workflows. When integration is poorly executed, it can cause significant operational disruptions. Systems that are not aligned with the broader infrastructure can lead to inefficiencies, data incompatibilities, and costly rework. Instead of enhancing operations, these poorly integrated AI systems can create bottlenecks, increase the complexity of workflows, and strain resources—ultimately becoming a burden rather than an asset.

Effective AI deployment requires careful planning to ensure compatibility with legacy systems, alignment with organizational goals, and the ability to adapt to evolving needs. Establishing robust communication between AI and existing platforms is crucial for data integrity, operational efficiency, and scalability.

- **Example**: An AI-powered resource planning tool failed to integrate with a company's legacy systems, resulting in significant data mismatches, operational inefficiencies, and increased manual work to reconcile information. Instead of streamlining processes, the AI system undermined its intended benefits and added complexity to daily operations.

11. Security Vulnerabilities

AI systems are increasingly becoming prime targets for cyberattacks. One major threat is adversarial attacks, where hackers manipulate input data to trick AI models into making incorrect decisions. This poses significant risks, especially in critical areas like autonomous vehicles, financial systems, and healthcare, where an AI failure can lead to dangerous or costly consequences.

These vulnerabilities not only threaten operational safety but also open the door to data breaches and system-wide disruptions. Ensuring robust security measures, such as regular monitoring and defensive protocols, is crucial to protecting AI systems from malicious attacks.

- **Example**: A public-facing AI chatbot was the victim of a targeted attack, where users intentionally manipulated its inputs, causing it to generate offensive messages.

12. Misaligned Objectives

AI systems are designed to optimize for specific objectives set by their creators. However, when these objectives are misaligned with broader societal values, ethical standards, or long-term consequences, the results can be harmful. AI may prioritize metrics like efficiency, engagement, or profitability without considering the potential negative effects on fairness, safety, or ethical considerations. This misalignment can lead to unintended behaviors, such as promoting harmful content, enabling biased decisions, or neglecting crucial safety measures.

One of the main challenges with AI is ensuring that its goals stay aligned with real-world values. If not properly managed, AI may exploit its objectives to achieve short-term gains at the cost of users' well-being or ethical standards. Designers must regularly review and adjust objectives to ensure responsible AI behavior.

- **Example**: An AI-driven recommendation system designed to maximize user engagement ended up promoting misleading or harmful content because it prioritized keeping users' attention over the quality or accuracy of the information. This misaligned objective had unintended consequences, leading to a spread of misinformation and a deterioration of trust among users.

13. Unrealistic Expectations, Hype, and Lack of Understanding Limitations

AI is often surrounded by hype and inflated expectations. While AI has the potential to solve complex problems, unrealistic expectations about its capabilities can lead to disappointment and failure when systems do not live up to their promises. Organizations may overestimate what AI can achieve, failing to fully understand its limitations and deficiencies, such as the model's inability to adapt to new data or environmental changes. Without proper safeguards to mitigate these limitations, AI systems can produce suboptimal or even harmful outcomes.

Furthermore, excessive hype can lead to poor planning and preparation, with companies rushing to deploy AI systems without addressing key challenges or implementing safeguards. This often results in high-profile failures that damage public perception of AI and cause long-term reputational harm.

- **Example**: An AI system promoted as a revolutionary tool for customer service automation was unable to handle the variety of real-world inquiries and failed to meet expectations due to its rigid limitations, ultimately leading to customer dissatisfaction and a loss of trust.

14. Ethical and Legal Failures

As AI continues to evolve, its rapid development often outpaces the creation of ethical guidelines and legal frameworks. Ethical and legal failures occur when AI systems are deployed in ways that violate individuals' rights or when the technology is used irresponsibly. Issues such as privacy violations, consent, and accountability are often overlooked, leading to unintended and sometimes harmful consequences.

The absence of robust regulations around AI means that companies can deploy systems without fully considering their societal or legal impact. This can result in lawsuits, public backlash, or violations of civil liberties.

- **Example**: A facial recognition system deployed in public spaces to enhance security raised concerns about surveillance and privacy violations, as individuals were being monitored without their consent.

15. Ethical Blind Spots (Fairness vs. Efficiency Trade-offs)

AI systems often face trade-offs between maximizing efficiency and ensuring fairness. When these systems prioritize efficiency—whether it's cost reduction, speed, or optimization—over ethical considerations like fairness or social impact, significant ethical blind spots can emerge. These blind spots are especially problematic when vulnerable communities or marginalized groups are affected, even if the AI system is technically functioning as intended.

The challenge is recognizing that efficiency gains aren't always beneficial if they compromise fairness. AI systems must balance optimization with ethical considerations, ensuring they don't marginalize individuals. Achieving this balance requires ongoing oversight to prevent harmful outcomes.

- **Example**: An AI-driven resource allocation system prioritized cost-cutting measures, which led to the inadvertent marginalization of vulnerable communities. By focusing solely on efficiency, the system ignored broader social impacts, resulting in unequal resource distribution and harm to those who were already disadvantaged

Conclusion: The Interconnected Nature of AI Failures

As we've seen, AI failures rarely result from a single cause. More often than not, they arise from a combination of factors that reinforce one another. For example, biased data can lead to discriminatory outcomes, which could have been prevented with proper human oversight or more transparent decision-making. Similarly, over-reliance on historical data often exacerbates unrealistic expectations, leading to failure when the real world diverges from past trends.

Addressing these failures requires a comprehensive approach. It's not enough to focus on just one aspect, like improving data quality or making algorithms more transparent. Instead, AI systems need to be built with a multi-layered strategy that includes robust data governance, fairness audits, explainability, security, and human oversight. By addressing these challenges holistically, AI developers can create systems that are more reliable, ethical, and adaptable.

These foundational principles are crucial to understanding the more specific case studies explored in later chapters. By recognizing how these core failure mechanisms manifest in different contexts, readers can gain a deeper appreciation for the complexity of AI failures and the solutions needed to prevent them.

Looking Ahead: Data Quality

In the next chapter, we will examine the role of data quality in AI systems. As demonstrated in this chapter, many AI failures can be traced back to poor data whether it's incomplete, outdated, or biased. We will explore how these data issues impact the performance of AI and lead to incidents across various industries and discuss strategies for improving data quality to reduce risks in AI deployment.

Chapter 3: Data Quality and Its Impact on AI Projects

Artificial intelligence (AI) systems rely heavily on data, and the quality of that data directly influences the effectiveness and reliability of their outputs. As British mathematician Clive Humby famously said, *"Data is the new oil"*—a powerful resource that fuels AI-driven innovation across industries. Whether used in product recommendations, healthcare decision-making, or predictive analytics, the success of AI hinges on receiving accurate, unbiased, and up-to-date data. The concept of "garbage in, garbage out" perfectly captures the risks AI systems face when fed with poor-quality data such as incomplete, biased, or outdated datasets. When AI models are trained on flawed data, they can generate erroneous insights, inaccurate predictions, and, in some cases, harmful decisions.

While AI's ability to process large volumes of data quickly has led to significant breakthroughs, this chapter examines cases where poor data quality resulted in notable failures. Examples include the flawed datasets in facial recognition technologies, like Amazon Rekognition's misidentification of members of Congress, and the failure of Google Flu Trends, which inaccurately predicted flu outbreaks due to skewed search data. These cases highlight the importance of proper data governance, continuous data validation, and the responsible use of data in ensuring the success and reliability of AI applications. Without addressing these issues, AI systems run the risk of amplifying biases, perpetuating errors, and ultimately delivering results that erode public trust.

Data quality must be a priority at every stage of AI development, from collection and preprocessing to continuous monitoring of inputs and outputs. Ensuring diverse datasets, addressing bias, and keeping data up-to-date are essential for unlocking AI's full potential while minimizing the risks posed by poor-quality inputs.

Case Study 1: Amazon's Facial Recognition Software Misidentifies Congresspeople with Criminal Mugshots

What Went Wrong:

In 2018, the American Civil Liberties Union (ACLU) conducted a high-profile test of Amazon's Rekognition, an AI-driven facial recognition tool, to assess its accuracy and potential implications for law enforcement use. The test involved running photos of U.S. members of Congress through the Rekognition system, comparing their faces against a database of 25,000 publicly available mugshots using the products default match settings. The result was shocking: twenty-eight members of Congress, including prominent figures such as civil rights leader John Lewis, were misidentified as criminals (ACLU, 2018).

Even more troubling was the fact that nearly 40% of those falsely identified were people of color, despite making up only about 20% of Congress. This alarming disparity highlighted the racial bias embedded in the system, raising concerns not just about the technology's accuracy but about its potential for misuse in policing, particularly in communities of color. The ACLU emphasized that this kind of error could have devastating consequences if used by law enforcement agencies to make arrests or inform criminal investigations, especially when disproportionately targeting minorities (ACLU, 2018).

Likely Cause of Failure:

Amazon Rekognition, like other facial recognition technologies, likely suffered from demographic bias due to the lack of balanced representation in its training data. Research has shown that facial recognition systems tend to perform poorly on certain demographics, particularly women and people with darker skin tones, when trained predominantly on lighter-skinned individuals. Studies have highlighted this imbalance in widely used facial recognition benchmarks like IJB-A and Adience, where lighter-skinned individuals make up 79.6% and 86.2% of the datasets, respectively. This lack of diversity leads to significantly higher error rates when identifying people with darker skin, particularly women of color (Buolamwini and Gebru, 2018).

In tests evaluating commercial facial analysis algorithms, error rates for darker-skinned females were notably higher up to 34.7% in some systems compared to lighter-skinned males, whose error rates were less than 1% (Buolamwini and Gebru, 2018). This suggests that Amazon's Rekognition could have faced similar issues due to the inherent bias in training datasets that are unrepresentative of the full range of skin tones and demographic characteristics, leading to misidentifications and lower accuracy when identifying people of color.

It's important to note that the ACLU conducted its test using Amazon Rekognition's default settings, which operate at an 80% confidence threshold. However, a spokeswoman for Amazon Web Services later clarified that when using the system for identifying individuals, they recommend adjusting the threshold to 95% or higher for greater accuracy (BBC News, 2018). This discrepancy in the recommended settings may have contributed to the misidentifications observed in the ACLU's test.

Lessons Learned:

This case underscores the importance of diversity in training datasets when developing AI systems, particularly those intended for high-stakes applications like law enforcement. When AI is used to identify individuals or make decisions that affect personal rights and freedoms, it is essential that the data reflects the diversity of the population it will serve. Failure to do so can result in biased outcomes that disproportionately affect marginalized groups, as seen with Amazon Rekognition.

Moreover, this incident highlights the need for rigorous testing and ongoing oversight before deploying AI systems in sensitive real-world environments. Law enforcement agencies, in particular, must exercise extreme caution when adopting facial recognition technology, as errors can lead to false arrests, wrongful detentions, and violations of civil rights. Ensuring that AI systems are independently tested for bias and accuracy across a wide range of demographic groups can help build public trust and reduce the risk of discriminatory outcomes.

Finally, this case emphasizes the broader societal and ethical implications of using AI systems like facial recognition in policing. Without proper regulation, transparency, and accountability, these technologies could exacerbate racial disparities and undermine public confidence in law enforcement institutions.

Case Study 2: Google Flu Trends' Failure Due to Data Quality Issues

What Went Wrong:

In 2008, Google launched Google Flu Trends (GFT), a project that aimed to predict flu outbreaks in real-time by analyzing large volumes of flu-related search queries. The premise was simple: by tracking how often people searched for flu symptoms, the system could predict flu activity across regions faster than traditional methods like those used by the Centers for Disease Control and Prevention (CDC). Initially, GFT showed promise and gained significant attention for its ability to process large-scale data for public health. The model developed to predict influenza-like illness (ILI) trends using search query data showed strong performance both during its training period and when tested on new data. From 2003 to 2007, the model achieved a mean correlation of 0.90 with CDC-reported flu percentages across nine regions, indicating a strong fit between the search data and actual flu cases. When tested on previously unseen data from 2007 to 2008, the model performed even better, with a mean correlation of 0.97. These results demonstrated the model's effectiveness in capturing flu trends based on search query data and its ability to generalize well to new data (Ginsberg et al., 2009).

However, by 2013, GFT was consistently overestimating the prevalence of flu cases. At its peak, the system was predicting double the actual number of flu cases reported by the CDC. The failure raised concerns about the reliability of search data as a sole indicator for flu outbreaks, especially when compared to verified medical reports (Lazer et al., 2014).

Likely Cause of Failure:

A 2014 study found that Google Flu Trends (GFT) consistently overestimated flu prevalence over several years, exposing fundamental issues rooted in both big data hubris and algorithm dynamics. GFT developers relied on an enormous volume of search data to predict flu outbreaks, assuming that the sheer quantity of data would lead to highly accurate predictions. The methodology involved matching 50 million search terms to just 1,152 data points (flu case reports from the CDC), creating a high risk of overfitting. This mismatch between the vast number of variables (search terms) and limited data points increased the likelihood of spurious correlations such as search terms for high school basketball being mistakenly linked to flu incidence because of seasonal patterns. Despite developers removing some clearly unrelated terms, the model still failed to generalize effectively and missed key events, such as the 2009 H1N1 pandemic. It continued to overestimate flu prevalence during the 2011-2013 seasons, highlighting the limitations of relying solely on big data without traditional validation and statistical methods (Lazer et al., 2014).

In addition to overfitting, Google Flu Trends (GFT) was heavily influenced by changes in Google's search algorithms, which were constantly updated to improve user experience and generate revenue. These changes unintentionally affected the accuracy of GFT's flu predictions. For instance, updates to Google's algorithms in 2011 and 2012 introduced features like suggested search terms and potential diagnoses for symptoms such as "fever" and "cough" (Lazer et al., 2014). These modifications likely caused users to search for terms that were not directly related to flu incidence but that influenced GFT's tracking, by increasing the prevalence of searches for treatments or ways to distinguish the flu from a common cold. This led to systematic errors in GFT, as the model was built on the assumption that search behavior was static and directly related to flu activity.

Additionally, by frequently updating the search algorithms, Google effectively altered the data feeding into the model from what it had originally been trained on. The model was developed based on specific search behaviors and patterns that were likely presumed to remain consistent over time. However, changes in how users searched prompted by algorithm updates meant the data stream was no longer aligned with the original model's training data. As a result, GFT began tracking flu-like behavior inaccurately, confusing shifts in user behavior with actual changes in flu prevalence.

Lessons Learned:

The failure of Google Flu Trends (GFT) provides several important lessons regarding the use of big data and the design of predictive models. First, big data alone is insufficient. GFT relied on vast amounts of search query data but lacked balance with traditional data sources, leading to overfitting. The model ended up correlating irrelevant search terms with flu outbreaks, resulting in flawed predictions. This highlights the need for predictive models to incorporate big data alongside traditional statistical methods, ensuring that models prioritize the quality and relevance of data over sheer quantity.

Another critical lesson is the importance of integrating both big and small data. While big data offers the ability to detect broad patterns, small data sources such as verified public health reports, hospital records, CDC flu reports, and patient surveys add vital context and precision. These traditional datasets provide validated, reliable information that can confirm or refute trends suggested by big data. GFT's overreliance on search data alone, without the inclusion of more reliable, verified information, contributed to its inaccuracies. Successful models must combine big data's scale with small data's precision to ensure more accurate outcomes.

Furthermore, GFT's errors were exacerbated by algorithm dynamics. Google's search algorithms were regularly updated, unintentionally altering the data fed into the model. These changes, such as introducing suggested search terms or potential diagnoses, led to shifts in user behavior that the model misinterpreted as changes in flu prevalence. This underscores the need for models to be adaptable and flexible, capable of adjusting to changes in how data is generated or collected over time.

Lastly, the GFT case emphasizes the need for models to account for data evolution. The static design of GFT couldn't adapt to shifts in user behavior or algorithm updates, leading to persistent inaccuracies. Models must be capable of adapting to dynamic inputs, ensuring their accuracy as data sources evolve.

Case Study 3: Google Photos AI Labeling Issue

What Went Wrong:

In 2015, Google Photos introduced an AI-driven image recognition system designed to automatically tag and categorize photos based on their content. The system was a major leap forward in photo management, eliminating the need for users to manually label their pictures. However, shortly after its launch, the AI system came under fire when it **misidentified images of African American individuals as "gorillas"**, a mistake that quickly garnered public outrage. This error not only damaged Google's reputation but also sparked a wider discussion about the reliability and fairness of AI systems (BBC News, 2015).

Why It Went Wrong:

This failure highlights the combined impact of algorithmic limitations and a lack of data diversity in the system's training. As detailed in the Wall Street Journal, the AI system, driven by machine learning, was unable to differentiate between offensive labels and more benign ones because it lacked contextual understanding. The algorithm likely made its best guess when uncertain, leading to offensive categorizations. This incident underscores the limitations of AI systems when they lack the capacity to recognize cultural sensitivities or differentiate between mistakes that may be acceptable and those that are harmful (The Wall Street Journal, 2015).

Beyond the algorithmic issues, this failure also highlights a broader issue of insufficient data diversity. Research by Buolamwini and Gebru (2018) found that many AI systems, are often trained primarily on data from Caucasian individuals, leaving the models ill-equipped to generalize across ethnic groups (Buolamwini and Gebru, 2018). It is likely, the lack of exposure to diverse skin tones and facial features during training impaired the system's ability to make accurate categorization of all ethnicities.

Moreover, the incident revealed the consequences of inadequate real-world testing. Google's system was deployed without sufficient testing across a diverse enough range of images, meaning it failed to account for errors when categorizing minority groups. Real-world testing is crucial for identifying such biases, as it exposes AI models to the kinds of variability they will encounter post-deployment. Without it, as seen in the Google Photos example, biases and errors may go unnoticed until they create significant public backlash

Lessons Learned:

The Google Photos incident in 2015 serves as a powerful reminder of the importance of diversity in training data and comprehensive real-world testing for AI models. One of the likely reasons for the mislabeling of Black individuals as "gorillas" was the lack of diverse images in the training data, which left the system ill-equipped to accurately categorize people with different skin tones and facial features. This failure illustrates that AI models can only be as effective and fair as the data they are trained on. When a system is trained predominantly on data from one demographic, it will likely struggle to perform accurately across underrepresented groups, perpetuating biases that exist in society.

Moreover, the incident highlights the importance of cultural sensitivity in AI models. Algorithms, by their nature, lack the ability to understand cultural contexts, making it essential for developers to anticipate and account for potential harmful mislabeling during development. This requires not only diverse data but also the inclusion of contextual awareness during the design of AI systems. Additionally, human oversight should be integrated into the testing process to address potential cultural misinterpretations or offensive categorizations.

Human reviewers can help flag issues that algorithms, operating without cultural context, might overlook. This would prevent harmful mislabeling, especially in sensitive areas such as racial or cultural identification.

Finally, the Google Photos failure underscores the need for extensive real-world testing. AI systems should be tested on diverse, real-world datasets that reflect the full spectrum of human diversity before being deployed. Testing AI models in such a manner can help identify and address biases early, preventing serious public backlash and ensuring that these systems work effectively for all users. The failure of Google Photos is a lesson in the risks of releasing AI technologies without sufficient testing, the need for human oversight, and the responsibility companies hold in ensuring that their systems are both inclusive and fair.

Advice for Preventing Data-Related AI Failures

At the core of many AI failures is poor data quality. To prevent similar mistakes in your AI projects, the following best practices can help ensure your systems are robust, reliable, and ethical:

1. **Use Diverse and Representative Datasets**: AI systems must be trained on data that reflects the full diversity of the real world. Ensuring that datasets are inclusive across factors like gender, race, geography, and socioeconomic status helps prevent bias and improves the accuracy of AI outputs. Without diversity in training data, AI systems risk producing skewed or inaccurate results when encountering underrepresented groups or unfamiliar scenarios.

2. **Continuous Data Governance**: Data quality must be maintained throughout the entire lifecycle of an AI system, not

just during its initial development. AI models must be regularly updated with fresh, relevant data to prevent them from becoming outdated or misaligned with current realities. Establishing robust data governance processes ensures that data is accurate, timely, and reflective of evolving conditions. Incorporating ongoing data feeds is crucial to keep the AI system constantly refreshed with new, real-time information, enabling it to adapt to changes in its environment.

3. Human Oversight: AI outputs should never be regarded as definitive. Human experts must continually review and validate AI-generated decisions, especially in high-stakes industries like healthcare, finance, and law enforcement. Human oversight is critical for identifying errors, biases, or unintended consequences that AI systems may not catch.

4. Test for Bias: Bias is often baked into AI systems through historical data. Therefore, before deployment, AI systems must undergo comprehensive testing for bias across different demographic groups. Regular bias audits help ensure that AI systems treat all users fairly and do not perpetuate discrimination or inequality.

5. Real-World Testing: Idealized or curated datasets often fail to capture the complexity of real-world environments. AI systems should be thoroughly stress-tested with real-world data to ensure they can handle varied and dynamic conditions. This type of testing helps reveal potential weaknesses in the system and ensures it can perform reliably in practice, not just in theory.

Conclusion: Data Is the Foundation of AI Success

As the case studies in this chapter demonstrate, data quality is the foundation upon which the success or failure of AI systems rests. Whether it is facial recognition software misidentifying individuals or a flu-tracking algorithm producing unreliable predictions, poor data quality can undermine even the most advanced AI technologies. These failures are not merely technical glitches; they can have profound ethical, social, and financial implications. When AI systems are built on incomplete, biased, or outdated datasets, they risk not only making inaccurate predictions but also perpetuating societal biases, eroding public trust, and causing significant harm to individuals and communities.

The case of Amazon Rekognition underscores the dangers of demographic bias and the importance of diverse training data in high-stakes applications like law enforcement. Similarly, Google Flu Trends illustrates how over-reliance on vast amounts of data, without proper validation or continuous updating, can lead to overfitting and flawed predictions. These examples highlight the need for careful data governance and ongoing data monitoring to ensure that AI systems remain accurate and aligned with real-world conditions.

To avoid these pitfalls, AI developers and organizations must prioritize the integrity of the data they use at every stage of the AI lifecycle. This includes ensuring that training datasets are diverse and representative, conducting rigorous testing for bias, and maintaining continuous oversight and updates to keep models relevant in dynamic environments. Human oversight remains a crucial element in validating AI decisions, particularly in areas where the stakes are high, such as healthcare, finance, and criminal justice. Failure to address these issues can result not only in technical setbacks but also in real-world harm, legal challenges, and damaged reputations.

Ultimately, the success of AI hinges on the quality, diversity, and relevance of the data it is fed. Without a solid data foundation, even the most sophisticated AI models can falter, leading to errors, misinterpretations, and unintended consequences. As AI becomes increasingly integrated into decision-making processes across industries, ensuring robust data governance will be critical to harnessing the full potential of these systems while minimizing risks. Companies and developers that prioritize data quality and ethical AI practices will not only improve the performance of their models but also build systems that are fair, transparent, and trustworthy.

Looking Ahead: Overfitting, Model Transparency, and AI's Responsiveness to Change

Data quality alone is not enough to ensure the success of AI systems. In the next chapter, we will focus on overfitting, transparency, and the ability of AI to respond to changing environments. Overfitting limits an AI model's ability to generalize beyond its training data, while a lack of transparency can lead to mistrust and poor oversight. We will explore these technical challenges and consider ways to build AI systems that are more adaptable, transparent, and reliable.

Chapter 4: Overfitting, Model Transparency, and AI's Responsiveness to Change

Artificial intelligence (AI) is transforming industries from healthcare to finance, offering innovative solutions that streamline decision-making processes and enable data-driven insights. However, despite its potential, AI is not without its limitations. Three critical challenges frequently cause AI systems to fail: overfitting and underfitting, lack of model transparency, and inability to adapt to rapidly changing conditions. These issues can lead to inaccurate predictions, loss of trust, financial losses, and broader societal harms.

Overfitting and Underfitting: The Balance of Generalization

At the core of many AI failures is the tension between overfitting and underfitting. When an AI model is overfitted, it becomes overly specialized to its training data, capturing patterns that may not exist in the real world. This results in an AI system that performs well on its training data but fails to generalize to new, unseen data. Overfitting often occurs when models are trained on too narrow a dataset or when they capture noise rather than meaningful patterns.

Conversely, underfitting occurs when a model is too simplistic, failing to capture important patterns in the data. Underfitted models tend to perform poorly both on the training data and in real-world scenarios because they haven't learned enough from the available data. Striking the right balance between overfitting and underfitting is crucial for building AI systems that are both accurate and flexible.

Both overfitting and underfitting highlight the importance of generalization. An AI model's ability to perform well across different datasets and real-world conditions. Poor generalization is a significant contributor to AI failures, especially in sectors like healthcare, finance, and retail, where conditions frequently change, and AI models must continuously adapt.

Model Transparency: The "Black Box" Problem

Another major issue facing AI development is the lack of transparency in many AI models, particularly those built on deep learning architectures. These models often operate as "black boxes," meaning their internal workings are so complex that even the developers who built them cannot fully explain how they arrive at specific decisions. This lack of explainability creates significant challenges, particularly in areas where AI systems are used to make high-stakes decisions, such as credit approvals, medical diagnoses, and criminal justice.

When an AI system cannot explain its decision-making process, it becomes difficult to assess whether its outputs are fair, accurate, or even legal. This opacity can lead to mistrust, regulatory challenges, and in some cases, accusations of bias or discrimination. Transparent AI models are essential not only for building trust with users but also for ensuring accountability and enabling human oversight.

Adaptability: AI's Struggle to Respond to Changing Environments

AI models are often trained on historical data, which may not reflect future conditions or emerging trends. Adaptability becomes crucial when AI systems are deployed in dynamic environments, such as real estate, finance, or public health, where conditions can shift rapidly due to external factors like pandemics, economic downturns, or regulatory changes. AI systems that cannot update or adapt in real-time are prone to making poor decisions that can result in significant financial or operational losses.

In volatile markets, for example, AI models that fail to adjust to new data can lead to overestimations or underestimations, causing businesses to lose competitive advantages. Adaptability, therefore, is key to ensuring that AI systems remain useful, relevant, and effective in real-world applications.

Case Study 1: Overfitting in COVID-19 Diagnosis Models

What Went Wrong:

During the COVID-19 pandemic, AI models were rapidly developed to diagnose and predict patient outcomes using chest radiographs (CXR) and computed tomography (CT) scans. While these models promised high accuracy, many were found to be deeply flawed due to overfitting on biased or poorly labeled datasets. One critical issue was the use of datasets that lacked diversity in patient demographics, medical conditions, and imaging quality. This led to models performing well in controlled test environments but failing to generalize in real-world clinical settings (Roberts et al., 2021).

A specific failure arose when models were trained on public datasets containing overlapping or low-quality images. Some datasets included pre-processed or compressed images from multiple sources, which reduced the models' ability to accurately diagnose COVID-19. In several instances, datasets contained duplicate images or irrelevant data from unrelated conditions. One glaring example involved models that were trained using data from adult COVID-19 patients but were compared with pediatric pneumonia datasets. The AI system then relied on recognizing the obvious differences between adult and pediatric patients—such as body size or lung shape—instead of focusing on the medical differences related to COVID-19. This artificial boost in performance masked the true diagnostic limitations of the model, leading to inflated accuracy claims (Roberts et al., 2021).

Ultimately, a review concluded that none of the machine learning models evaluated were suitable for clinical translation, indicating that the models' performance did not meet the rigorous standards necessary for real-world diagnosis and prognosis of COVID-19 (Roberts et al., 2021).

Why It Went Wrong:

The probable cause of failure was the overfitting of AI models to biased, non-representative, and low-quality datasets. In the rush to develop diagnostic tools, researchers did not sufficiently validate these models on diverse and external datasets. Many models were internally validated, using the same dataset for both training and testing, without cross-validation on external data sources, reinforcing overfitting and limiting generalizability.

A critical issue arose from the use of public datasets that contained overlapping or poorly labeled images. These datasets often included duplicate images or images unrelated to COVID-19, leading models to focus on irrelevant features, such as distinguishing between adult and pediatric patients, rather than diagnosing the disease itself. This artificially inflated the models' performance, masking their true limitations (Roberts et al., 2021).

Furthermore, the use of transfer learning, where models pre-trained on unrelated tasks were fine-tuned for COVID-19 diagnosis introduced additional complications. These models, originally designed for general image classification, were not optimized for the complexities of medical imaging (Roberts et al., 2021). This could lead to potential overfitting on superficial features of the images rather than meaningful clinical insights.

Lessons Learned:

This case highlights the critical importance of rigorous data selection, thorough validation, and robust testing practices in AI development. To prevent overfitting, it is essential that AI models are trained on large, diverse, and representative datasets that reflect the varied real-world conditions they will be applied to. Without such diversity, models may perform well in controlled environments but fail when deployed in broader, more complex scenarios. Additionally, external validation is crucial for ensuring that models can generalize effectively across different patient populations, avoiding over-reliance on internal validation, which can lead to overly optimistic performance estimates.

Equally important is the need for transparency in dataset composition and model training methodologies. Providing clear documentation of the data used and the methods employed in model development is vital to avoid misleading performance claims and to allow for independent verification and improvement. Openness and clarity in these areas help build trust in AI systems and ensure that they are evaluated properly before being deployed in real-world situations.

As demonstrated in this case, the urgency of deploying AI during a crisis must not come at the expense of model quality or reliability. Even when speed is a priority, it is essential to ensure that the models being developed are robust, accurate, and suitable for practical use.

Case Study 2: Lack of Model Transparency in Apple Card's Credit Decisions

What Went Wrong:

In 2019, Apple launched the Apple Card, a credit card using advanced algorithms to determine credit limits and approvals. However, the system quickly came under scrutiny after high-profile cases of alleged gender bias emerged. Several prominent individuals, including a tech entrepreneur, reported that their wives had been granted significantly lower credit limits despite having comparable financial profiles. These revelations led to investigations by regulators, who were concerned that the automated decision-making process could be discriminating against women in its credit assessments (The New York Times, 2019).

Apple co-founder Steve Wozniak posted on X that his wife had a similar experience and called for an investigation by the government into the use of such black box algorithms (The Vege, 2019). In a statement Goldman Sachs, which administered the card for Apple, denied that the algorithm would discriminate based on gender (The Verge, 2019).

This lack of transparency made it impossible for consumers to assess whether the algorithm was biased or flawed. Without a clear explanation of the model's logic, trust in the system eroded rapidly, leading to public outcry and regulatory scrutiny. In response to the complaints, the New York State Department of Financial Services (NYDFS) said it would investigate the card, which is issued by banking giant Goldman Sachs (The Verge, 2019).

Why It Went Wrong:

After reviewing approximately 400,000 credit applications, the NYDFS found no evidence of gender bias or unlawful discrimination under fair lending laws. In terms of gender, the Department found, based on its data analysis, that Apple Card applications from women and men with similar credit characteristics generally had similar outcomes (New York Department of Financial Services, 2021). However, they found deficiencies in customer service and a perceived lack of transparency, which undermined consumer trust in fair credit decisions. Goldman Sachs and Apple have since taken steps to improve transparency, implemented a program to assist denied applicants in improving their credit with the goal of obtaining Apple Card approval, and modified a policy that previously required approved applicants to wait six months before appealing credit terms . (New York Department of Financial Services, 2021).

This case clearly highlights the issues that can arise from a lack of transparency in an AI system's decision-making process. The complexity of the algorithm likely made its inner workings opaque, even to the developers. In high-stakes industries like finance, explainability is crucial for ensuring that consumers and regulators trust that decisions are made fairly. The failure to provide this transparency not only damaged the reputation of the companies involved but also underscored the broader risks of deploying black-box systems in critical areas, such as creditworthiness assessments.

Lessons Learned:

This case underscores the importance of building transparency into automated decision-making systems, especially when they are responsible for decisions that significantly impact people's lives. In sectors like finance, where fairness and accountability are paramount, such models must be explainable, auditable, and capable of providing clear reasoning for their decisions. When a system lacks transparency, it can lead to mistrust and potential legal challenges, even if the model itself is unbiased. The mere perception of unfairness or the inability to understand how decisions are made can erode consumer trust and invite regulatory scrutiny. Ensuring that these systems are designed with explainability from the outset is essential not only for maintaining consumer confidence but also for protecting against reputational damage and ensuring compliance with evolving legal standards.

Case Study 3: Lack of Adaptability in Zillow's AI Home-Buying Algorithm

What Went Wrong:

In 2018, Zillow, the real estate giant, launched **Zillow Offers**, an ambitious program that used AI to purchase homes directly from sellers, renovate them, and then sell them at a profit. Zillow's proprietary AI algorithm, known for generating its home price estimates or "Zestimates," was at the core of this new business model (Wired, 2021). The system used historical data to determine the value of homes and make competitive offers. However, by 2021, the housing market had become highly volatile, largely due to pandemic-related disruptions. The Zillow Offers algorithm, which largely relied on historical pre-pandemic data, began making poor predictions and overpaying for homes (Wired, 2021).

Zillow's AI system was unable to adapt to the rapid changes in the housing market, leading the company to purchase homes at inflated prices while struggling to resell them. The financial losses mounted, and by late 2021, Zillow announced that it was shutting down its home-buying program, taking a $540 million write-down on the project and reducing staff by 25% (CNN, 2021).

Why It Went Wrong:

The likely drivers behind the failure of Zillow's AI model can be attributed to several factors:

- **Inability to adapt to rapidly changing market conditions during the pandemic**: The unprecedented volatility caused by COVID-19 dramatically altered housing demand, with significant fluctuations that the AI model was not designed to handle. The AI, which relied on historical data and more stable market conditions, could not adjust quickly enough to account for the pandemic's rapid shifts in housing prices and buyer behavior.

- **Missing home features and attributes not captured by the model**: Many critical home attributes that could significantly impact the final valuation, such as interior conditions, renovations, or unique features, were not always reflected in Zillow's data. This omission limited the accuracy of the model's predictions, leading to skewed valuations that did not match the realities of the properties being analyzed.
- **Model's application on non-cookie-cutter homes**: Zillow's algorithm was designed to work best on standard, "cookie-cutter" homes that fit predictable patterns. When applied to more unique properties with atypical features or non-standard designs, the model struggled to generate accurate valuations due to its limited capacity to understand deviations from the norm (Wired, 2021; Stanford Graduate School of Business, 2021).

Zillow's AI model lacked the adaptability necessary to cope with rapidly changing market conditions, especially during the pandemic, and the human oversight in place was not sufficient to mitigate this deficiency. As the algorithm operated, it struggled to adjust to sudden shifts in housing demand and price fluctuations, leading to overinflated offers and significant financial losses. The lack of human intervention failed to address the model's shortcomings in real time, further compounding the problem.

Lessons Learned:

This case highlights the vital need for AI systems that are not only highly automated but also adaptable to dynamic, fast-changing environments. In markets like real estate, where sudden shifts can disrupt even the most data-driven decisions, relying solely on historical data can lead to significant errors. To avoid these pitfalls, AI models must be designed to integrate real-time inputs and undergo continuous monitoring and recalibration to stay relevant as conditions evolve. Flexibility is key to ensuring that the models do not become outdated in the face of rapid market changes or other unforeseen factors.

Equally critical is the role of human oversight. While AI excels at processing large volumes of data quickly and identifying patterns, it often lacks the nuance and contextual understanding required to make complex decisions in unpredictable environments. Human judgment complements AI, ensuring that errors, anomalies, or shifts in market dynamics that the model alone cannot anticipate are identified and addressed. By blending robust AI adaptability with vigilant human oversight, organizations can better navigate volatile environments, catching potential risks early and adjusting strategies accordingly. This approach not only strengthens decision-making but also ensures AI systems remain effective and responsive in real-world scenarios.

Advice for Preventing AI Failures in Overfitting, Transparency, and Adaptability

These case studies reveal key areas where AI systems often fail and offer valuable lessons for preventing similar mistakes in future projects. To build robust, reliable, and trustworthy AI systems, it is crucial to consider the following best practices:

1. **Addressing Overfitting and Underfitting**: Finding the balance between overfitting and underfitting is essential. AI systems should be trained on broad, diverse datasets to avoid overfitting, ensuring they can generalize effectively. This helps prevent the system from becoming overly tailored to a specific dataset or environment, which can limit its real-world application. On the other hand, underfitting where the model is too simplistic and fails to capture important patterns can lead to

equally poor performance. Striking this balance ensures that AI systems are both accurate and flexible enough to handle diverse scenarios.

2. Ensuring Data Diversity and Broad Generalization: AI systems must be trained on diverse datasets that reflect the variety of real-world scenarios they will encounter. This helps prevent overfitting and ensures that the AI can generalize effectively across different environments and populations. In dynamic industries like healthcare and real estate, continuous retraining on new data is essential to avoid the pitfalls of static models.

3. Prioritize Explainability and Transparency: Building transparency into AI systems from the outset is critical, especially in high-stakes applications like finance, healthcare, and law enforcement. Explainable AI (XAI) tools can help make decision-making processes more transparent, allowing developers, users, and regulators to understand how and why an AI system arrives at its conclusions. This transparency is vital for building trust and ensuring that AI systems operate fairly.

4. Design for Adaptability and Responsiveness: AI systems should be designed to handle changes in real-world conditions. This requires incorporating real-time data and feedback loops to ensure that models can adjust to new circumstances quickly. In volatile markets, such as real estate or stock trading, adaptability is crucial to avoid the risks of basing predictions solely on historical data. Human oversight can further enhance adaptability by providing context and judgment that AI systems may lack.

5. Continuous Monitoring and Updating: AI models should not be viewed as static entities. Continuous monitoring is necessary to ensure that the model's performance remains accurate and relevant over time. Regular updates and recalibrations based on real-world feedback and human oversight can prevent models from becoming obsolete, particularly in rapidly changing environments.

Conclusion: The Interconnected Nature of AI Failures

The challenges of overfitting, lack of transparency, and poor adaptability in AI systems are not isolated problems. As seen in the case studies throughout this chapter, these failures often intersect, creating a cascading effect that undermines the efficacy of AI in real-world applications. Overfitting hampers a model's ability to generalize beyond its training data, which becomes especially problematic in rapidly changing environments. At the same time, the lack of transparency makes it difficult for users, regulators, and even developers to trust or understand the decisions made by these systems. When combined with a lack of adaptability, AI systems risk becoming static, failing to evolve with new data or trends, and ultimately leading to significant financial, operational, and societal consequences.

To build robust AI systems capable of long-term success, developers must embrace a more holistic approach. This involves more than just focusing on technical optimization; it requires the incorporation of diverse, representative datasets to prevent overfitting, prioritizing transparency to build trust, and ensuring adaptability to stay relevant in dynamic environments. Moreover, continuous monitoring, recalibration, and human oversight are essential in mitigating the risks posed by these AI limitations.

In the rapidly evolving landscape of AI, ensuring these systems remain flexible, accountable, and transparent will be critical for their integration into key industries such as healthcare, finance, and beyond.

Only by addressing these interconnected failures can we unlock the full potential of AI to transform industries, improve decision-making, and foster innovation responsibly.

Looking Ahead: Algorithmic Bias and Discrimination

Overfitting and transparency may be technical challenges, but another critical issue is algorithmic bias. In the next chapter, we will explore how AI systems can unintentionally amplify societal biases when trained on biased data. From racial profiling in facial recognition to biased hiring algorithms, we will investigate how bias manifests in AI and offer solutions for creating fairer, more equitable systems.

Chapter 5: Algorithmic Bias and Discrimination

Artificial intelligence (AI) is often seen as a tool to eliminate human biases, bringing fairness and objectivity to processes that have historically been prone to discrimination, such as hiring, lending, and criminal justice. However, the reality is that AI, when trained on biased data or designed without careful oversight, can replicate, and even amplify existing societal biases. This phenomenon, known as algorithmic bias, occurs when AI systems disproportionately favor, or disadvantage particular groups based on attributes like race, gender, or socioeconomic status. As shown in the harm distribution bias chart in Chapter 1, this is a real problem that is still occurring and impacting people.

Algorithmic bias can manifest in several ways. For instance, an AI system might unfairly penalize women during job application processes, as seen with Amazon's AI recruiting tool. Similarly, credit-scoring algorithms may inadvertently provide lower limits to women or minorities, exacerbating financial inequality. These biases are often unintentional, resulting from historical data patterns embedded in the algorithms. Nevertheless, their impact can be far-reaching and detrimental to those affected.

In this chapter, we explore how AI systems, once touted as neutral and objective, have sometimes perpetuated discrimination. We will examine several high-profile examples of algorithmic bias, analyzing what went wrong, why it happened, and the lessons that can be drawn from these failures. By understanding these pitfalls, we can work towards building AI systems that are fairer, more transparent, and accountable.

Case Study 1: Amazon's AI Recruiting Tool

What Went Wrong:

In 2018, Amazon's AI-driven recruiting tool made headlines for all the wrong reasons. The company developed the tool to streamline its hiring process by automatically reviewing and ranking job applicants based on their resumes. This AI system was supposed to reduce the time it took to sift through hundreds of applications and identify the top candidates. However, it soon became evident that the tool was biased against female candidates. The algorithm systematically downgraded resumes that included the word "women's," such as "women's chess club," and favored resumes that used more traditionally male-dominated terms like "executed" or "captured" (Reuters, 2018).

Women applying for technical roles were particularly affected, as the AI devalued their resumes compared to those of men, even when they had comparable skills and experience. As a result, male candidates were consistently ranked higher, reinforcing the gender imbalances that Amazon's hiring processes were initially designed to overcome (The Guardian, 2018b).

Why It Went Wrong:

Amazon's recruiting tool was trained on resumes submitted to the company over a ten-year period. However, the majority of these resumes came from men, particularly in technical fields, where gender disparities have long been an issue. As a result, the AI, learning from this biased historical data, began to favor the same patterns, resulting in biased outcomes. The algorithm effectively "learned" that men were more likely to be hired for technical roles and began ranking male candidates higher.

This bias manifested in several ways. For instance, the tool penalized resumes that included the word "women's," such as "women's chess club captain," and downgraded graduates from two all-women's colleges, though the names of these schools were not disclosed. The algorithm also favored resumes containing verbs more commonly found on male engineers' applications, such as "executed" and "captured." In addition to the gender bias, the AI faced broader issues with data quality. The flawed data caused the system to recommend unqualified candidates for various positions, and at times, it returned results almost at random. Ultimately, due to these inconsistent and unreliable outcomes, Amazon decided to shut down the project (Reuters, 2018).

The likely cause of this failure was a lack of diverse data and an over-reliance on historical trends, which perpetuated existing biases rather than challenging them. Furthermore, Amazon did not implement sufficient bias checks or model adjustments to address the inherent biases present in the data. Without these corrective mechanisms, the algorithm continued to reflect and reinforce the biases it had learned. By the time the bias was discovered, the tool had already been in use, affecting applicants.

Lessons Learned:

This case highlights the critical importance of designing AI systems with fairness, inclusivity, and accountability in mind. Training AI systems on diverse and balanced datasets is essential, especially when those systems are responsible for decisions that significantly impact people's lives, such as hiring. If historical biases are embedded in the training data, AI models will replicate and reinforce these biases unless actively corrected. The Amazon case demonstrates how easily AI can exacerbate systemic issues if proper safeguards are not in place.

To avoid such outcomes, regular bias audits and testing should be built into every stage of the AI development process. It's not enough to simply rely on past data; developers must continually assess and address potential sources of bias. Bias detection tools and corrective algorithms must be implemented to ensure that models evolve with fairness and inclusivity in mind. For instance, incorporating fairness metrics during model training and evaluation can help to detect disparities early and prevent them from influencing the AI's decision-making processes.

Additionally, the case underscores the need for transparent oversight throughout the AI lifecycle. While AI can significantly improve the speed and efficiency of tasks like resume screening, it is critical to balance this automation with human oversight to ensure ethical standards are upheld. AI systems, particularly in sensitive areas like recruitment, should never be allowed to operate in isolation. Human judgment must remain central to the decision-making process to ensure that final outcomes are both fair and equitable.

Finally, this case emphasizes the value of cross-functional collaboration between data scientists, ethicists, and HR professionals. Developing AI should be seen not only as a technical challenge but as an ethical one, requiring diverse expertise to ensure that the technology reflects societal values. Companies adopting AI in high-impact areas must proactively address ethical concerns, ensuring that their systems actively work to dismantle, rather than perpetuate, existing inequalities.

Case Study 2: Google Gemini's Over-Correction in Bias

What Went Wrong:

In 2023, Google released its Gemini AI, an advanced language model that aimed to address previous concerns about bias and fairness in AI-generated content. However, shortly after its release, Gemini came under scrutiny for being "overly woke" in its responses. The system, which was designed to be sensitive to issues surrounding inclusivity and fairness, was found to produce responses that overemphasized gender and racial inclusivity in ways that sometimes felt excessive or out of context to users (BBC, 2024).

For example, Google's Gemini AI generated historically inaccurate images, such as Black Nazis, an Asian man among America's Founding Fathers, and Black depictions of George Washington. These distortions were attempts to promote inclusivity, but they led to widespread frustration. Users criticized the AI's bias correction mechanisms, arguing that they were too interventionist and compromised historical accuracy and neutrality. The backlash highlighted concerns that Gemini's approach to addressing bias overshadowed its effectiveness in delivering relevant and factual content (AFR, 2024).

Why It Went Wrong:

It appears that Google's Gemini AI encountered issues because, in trying to correct for bias, it created a new problem: outputs that were overly politically correct, sometimes to the point of absurdity. This likely stemmed from the large amounts of publicly available data the AI was trained on, which inherently contains biases. For example, traditional images of doctors often depict men, while images of cleaners tend to feature women. Previous AI systems trained on such data made mistakes, such as not recognizing Black faces or assuming only men held high-powered jobs (BBC, 2024). Google, in particular, had a history of such missteps, as its photos app once infamously mislabelled Black people as gorillas (BBC News, 2015).

To counteract these biases, Google appears to have given Gemini instructions to avoid making such assumptions. However, this overcorrection backfired, as the AI struggled with the nuances of human history and culture. For example, AI systems need specific programming to know that historical figures like the Founding Fathers or Nazis weren't Black. Without such understanding, the AI produced historically inaccurate outputs (BBC, 2024).

Experts like Dr. Sasha Luccioni noted that fixing these problems is complex, as there is no straightforward answer for what the outputs should be. She suggested user input as a potential solution, though this presents its own challenges. Additionally, Professor Alan Woodward pointed out that the bias issue is likely deeply embedded in both the training data and the algorithms, making it difficult to unpick. He emphasized the need for human oversight in any system where AI output is considered the "ground truth" (BBC, 2024).

This issue highlights two primary problems. First, overfitting to a specific social goal (in this case, inclusivity) led to imbalanced AI behavior. By overemphasizing fairness and inclusivity, the model ended up creating responses that alienated some users, as it failed to maintain a balance between correcting bias and delivering neutral, effective answers. Second, there was insufficient real-world testing and feedback integration. If Google had conducted broader testing with a more diverse set of users, it could have identified this issue earlier and made adjustments to the AI's language processing.

Lessons Learned:

The Google Gemini case underscores the importance of balancing bias correction with other key aspects of AI performance, such as relevance, clarity, and neutrality. While it is crucial to address harmful biases in AI, overcompensating in one direction can introduce new forms of bias or cause user dissatisfaction, as seen in Gemini's overly woke responses. Developers must ensure that AI models strike a balance between fairness and effective communication, while avoiding extremes that distort outputs.

Moreover, this case highlights the need for real-world user testing, continuous feedback loops, and robust human oversight. AI systems must be tested in diverse, practical scenarios to assess how users respond to bias correction mechanisms. Human intervention is crucial to ensure that AI outputs align with both factual accuracy and user expectations. In Google's case, a more balanced approach that included human oversight and user feedback could have prevented the AI from over-correcting its responses to the point where they no longer felt relevant or neutral. By integrating human judgment into the loop, developers can catch and correct missteps before they reach users.

Advice for Preventing Algorithmic Bias in AI

The presence of bias in AI systems is a critical issue, particularly when these technologies influence decisions about hiring, lending, or access to crucial resources, perpetuating societal inequalities if left unchecked. To prevent algorithmic bias from harming individuals and perpetuating societal inequalities, the following best practices can be implemented:

1. **Use Diverse and Representative Training Data**: AI systems must be trained on data that is representative of all demographic groups. This ensures that the algorithm does not disproportionately favor one group over another.

2. **Conduct Bias Audits**: Regular audits should be performed to test AI systems for bias. This involves running the system on test cases representing different genders, races, and other demographic variables to ensure fair treatment across all groups.

3. **Increase Transparency in AI Decision-Making**: AI systems should be designed with transparency in mind, allowing developers and stakeholders to understand how decisions are made. Black box models are particularly dangerous in high-stakes areas like hiring and lending.

4. **Incorporate Human Oversight**: AI should support human decision-making, not replace it. In critical areas like hiring,

finance, and healthcare, human experts should always review AI-generated outputs to ensure fairness and accuracy.

5. **Implement Feedback Loops for Continuous Improvement**: AI systems should have mechanisms for continuous feedback and improvement. If bias is detected, the model should be retrained with more representative data to ensure fairer outcomes.

Conclusion: The Importance of Fair and Transparent AI

The case studies and discussions throughout this chapter and book highlight the profound risks that algorithmic bias poses to both individuals and broader society. From hiring processes that disadvantage women to financial systems that reinforce racial disparities, the unintended consequences of AI can entrench existing inequalities if not vigilantly addressed.

However, these examples also offer a roadmap for improvement. Ensuring fairness in AI demands a proactive approach, starting with the data used to train these models. Diverse, representative datasets can help prevent AI from perpetuating historical biases, while regular bias audits provide a vital mechanism for identifying and correcting skewed outcomes. Beyond the technical fixes, human oversight is essential, ensuring that AI supports rather than overrides ethical decision-making, especially in high-stakes areas like employment, lending, and criminal justice.

Ultimately, the goal is not just to mitigate bias but to build AI systems that foster equity and inclusivity. Achieving this requires more than just sophisticated technology; it calls for a commitment to transparency, continuous feedback loops, and the involvement of diverse voices at every stage of AI development. With the right safeguards in place, we can harness the power of AI to enhance fairness rather than perpetuate discrimination, creating a future where these technologies better serve everyone.

Looking Ahead: Over-Reliance on AI and Lack of Human Oversight

In the next chapter, we will explore another key issue in AI development: over-reliance on AI systems and the lack of human oversight. While AI can automate complex tasks and make predictions at scale, relying too heavily on AI without human intervention can lead to catastrophic failures. We will examine high-profile cases where AI made critical errors due to the absence of sufficient human oversight and offer insights on how to maintain the right balance between AI and human control.

Chapter 6: Over-Reliance on AI and Lack of Human Oversight

Artificial intelligence (AI) has revolutionized industries, from manufacturing and transportation to healthcare and finance. Its ability to automate complex tasks, analyze massive datasets, and make real-time decisions has led to unprecedented efficiencies. However, the excitement around AI's capabilities has often led to an overestimation of its infallibility. Many believe that AI can replace human judgment entirely, trusting these systems to handle critical operations with minimal intervention. This over-reliance on AI can have disastrous consequences, particularly in high-stakes environments where errors can lead to significant financial losses, reputational damage, or even human casualties.

While AI can significantly enhance productivity, it is not without limitations. Algorithms are trained on data, which may not always capture every possible scenario. Furthermore, AI systems can malfunction or produce unintended outcomes in unfamiliar situations. These risks become amplified when human oversight is reduced or removed entirely.

In this chapter, we will explore several high-profile failures caused by over-reliance on AI systems and the lack of sufficient human oversight. These case studies highlight the dangers of assuming that AI can replace human judgment, particularly in critical industries like aviation and autonomous driving. The lessons learned from these incidents underscore the importance of maintaining a balance between automation and human control, ensuring that AI serves as a tool to support, rather than replace, human decision-making.

Case Study 1: Boeing 737 Max Crashes

What Went Wrong:

The Boeing 737 Max crashes in 2018 and 2019 were two of the deadliest aviation disasters in modern history, resulting in the deaths of 346 people. These tragedies were caused, in part, by a faulty system known as the Maneuvering Characteristics Augmentation System (MCAS). The MCAS was designed to automatically correct the plane's nose angle if it detected that the aircraft was climbing too steeply, thereby preventing a stall. However, the system relied on input from a single sensor to gauge the plane's angle of attack. When this sensor malfunctioned, it triggered the MCAS to push the nose of the plane downward repeatedly, despite the pilots' attempts to regain control (RSNA, 2020; News.com.au, 2020).

The key issue was that the MCAS overrode the pilots' manual inputs, continuously pushing the aircraft into a dive based on faulty data. The pilots were unaware of how the system worked and were not sufficiently trained on how to disable it in an emergency. As a result, they were left helpless as the MCAS system caused the planes to crash.

Why It Went Wrong:

Boeing's over-reliance on the MCAS system, combined with inadequate pilot training, was a major factor in the 737 MAX disasters. The MCAS was introduced to enhance the aircraft's handling by automatically adjusting the horizontal stabilizer in certain flight conditions to prevent stalls. However, Boeing failed to adequately account for potential system malfunctions or erroneous sensor data. A critical design flaw was the MCAS system's dependence on a single Angle of Attack (AOA) sensor to determine when to activate. This lack of redundancy meant that if the AOA sensor provided faulty data, as it did in both accidents, the MCAS would repeatedly and erroneously push the aircraft's nose down, leading to a loss of control.

The Federal Aviation Administration's (FAA) findings revealed that the MCAS had the ability to exert substantial control over the aircraft, more than was originally understood by many of the pilots. Because the system was triggered by only one AOA sensor and there was no cross-checking with a secondary sensor, it continuously operated based on incorrect data, causing the aircraft to dive repeatedly. The pilots, unaware of the system's full functionality and lacking clear procedures for how to override it, struggled to regain control (Federal Aviation Administration, 2020).

Additionally, the FAA report highlights that the training provided to pilots on the MCAS system was insufficient. The pilots were not given comprehensive information about how the system operated or the correct procedures to follow in the event of a malfunction. Without this knowledge, pilots were unable to effectively respond to the MCAS-induced nose-down conditions, contributing to the tragic outcomes (Federal Aviation Administration, 2020).

The decision to rely heavily on automation, without building in sufficient redundancies or clear manual override mechanisms, was a critical error. The dependence on a single sensor for crucial flight data, combined with insufficient pilot training, underscores the risks of relying on automated systems without the necessary safeguards.

Lessons Learned:

The Boeing 737 MAX crashes offer important general lessons about the risks of over-relying on automation without proper safeguards across various industries. First, automated systems must be designed with multiple layers of redundancy to ensure they can function safely even in the event of a sensor failure or incorrect data input. Relying on a single source of information, as seen with the Angle of Attack (AOA) sensor, can lead to catastrophic outcomes when that data is faulty. This principle applies to any system where automation is used to make critical decisions.

Second, human oversight remains essential. No matter how advanced the technology, automated systems should always have clear and accessible fail-safes that allow human operators to intervene quickly in case of malfunctions. Automation should support, not replace, human judgment, especially in high-stakes environments where errors can have severe consequences. Ensuring that operators have the ability and authority to override the system is key to maintaining safety and reliability.

Finally, training and transparency are vital. Operators must be fully trained in all aspects of the automated system, including how it works and how to disable or adjust it in case of an emergency. Inadequate training can leave users unprepared to respond when automation fails. This applies not just in aviation, but across industries such as healthcare, manufacturing, and finance, where complex systems interact with human decision-making.

Case Study 2: Uber's Self-Driving Car Fatality

What Went Wrong:

In 2018, a tragic incident occurred during the testing of Uber's autonomous vehicle when a self-driving car struck and killed a pedestrian in Tempe, Arizona, marking the first known fatality caused by an autonomous vehicle in the United States. The Uber test vehicle was operating in self-driving mode with a human safety driver behind the wheel. However, the driver was distracted and not paying attention, and the vehicle failed to detect the pedestrian crossing the street (The Verge, 2018).

In 2023, Rafaela Vasquez, the Uber safety driver involved in the accident, was sentenced to three years of supervised probation after pleading guilty to endangerment. A National Transportation Safety Board (NTSB) investigation found that the crash could have been avoided if the driver had been attentive. Vasquez, who was distracted by a video on her smartphone, and did not intervene when the vehicle struck the pedestrian (CNN, 2023).

The investigation also revealed that Uber's self-driving software wasn't designed to anticipate pedestrians crossing outside designated crosswalks, contributing to the vehicle's failure to respond in time (CNN, 2023). This case underscores the continued responsibility of human operators when supervising semi-autonomous vehicles, even with advanced features like radar cruise control and lane-keeping assistance. It highlights the importance of human oversight in ensuring the safety of both passengers and pedestrians.

Why It Went Wrong:

The fatality was the result of a combination of technological failure and human negligence. Uber's self-driving system struggled to correctly interpret complex, real-world scenarios. Although the vehicle's sensors detected the pedestrian, the AI system did not make the correct decision to avoid the collision. The NTSB investigation concluded that Uber's Advanced Technologies Group (ATG) failed to properly manage the limitations of its self-driving system, particularly its inability to predict and classify pedestrians crossing outside of crosswalks. This system failure was a key factor in the fatal accident. Additionally, the decision to disable the vehicle's emergency braking function, without implementing alternative safety measures, significantly increased the risks during testing. The removal of critical safety features, such as forward collision warning and automatic emergency braking, eliminated essential redundancies, contributing to the crash (National Transportation Safety Board, 2019).

This case highlighted the dangers of relying on autonomous systems without ensuring that human oversight is actively maintained. Although a human safety driver was present, they were distracted and failed to intervene when necessary. Uber's system placed too much confidence in the AI to handle complex situations, assuming that the human driver would intervene only as a last resort. However, this assumption broke down when the driver was not paying attention, leading to a failure of both the AI and human elements to prevent the crash.

Lessons Learned:

The Uber self-driving car fatality serves as a stark reminder of the critical need for continuous human oversight in autonomous systems, especially when those systems are still in development or testing. This case demonstrates that even advanced AI systems are not foolproof and can struggle with real-world complexities. Human operators must remain actively engaged, even in situations where the vehicle is handling most tasks autonomously. The assumption that human drivers will only intervene as a last resort proved flawed in this instance, as the distracted safety driver failed to prevent the tragedy. Ensuring that human drivers are fully aware of their responsibilities and are equipped to take over when necessary is essential to the safe deployment of autonomous technologies.

Moreover, this incident highlights the importance of fail-safe mechanisms in autonomous vehicles. Uber's decision to disable critical safety features, such as automatic emergency braking and forward collision warnings, significantly increased the risk during testing. Future autonomous systems must be equipped with reliable redundant safety measures that can take over when the AI fails, ensuring that there is always a backup plan in place to avoid catastrophic outcomes. These fail-safes should not be optional but a mandatory part of any semi-autonomous system to ensure passenger, pedestrian, and driver safety.

Another important lesson is the balance between AI trust and human vigilance. Autonomous technology has immense potential, but the human element cannot be disregarded. Developers and operators must be cautious about placing too much confidence in AI systems to handle unpredictable, real-world scenarios. This case highlights the dangers of over-reliance on autonomous systems without maintaining active human oversight to catch errors or misjudgments that AI alone may not be equipped to handle.

Finally, the legal and ethical implications of autonomous vehicle operations are crucial considerations. The fact that the safety driver in this incident faced criminal charges underscores that legal accountability still applies, even when a machine is doing the driving. Human operators can be held liable for accidents involving autonomous vehicles, making it critical that they remain fully engaged and prepared to act in the event of an emergency. This case demonstrates the need for clear legal frameworks and guidelines governing the use of autonomous vehicles, particularly as these technologies become more widespread.

Case Study 3: Tesla Autopilot Crash

What Went Wrong:

On March 23, 2018, a Tesla Model X P100D, traveling on US Highway 101 in Mountain View, California, collided with a previously damaged crash attenuator at a high speed of 71 mph. As the vehicle approached the gore area dividing the main lanes from an exit ramp, it veered into this section and struck the nonoperational crash attenuator. The impact caused severe damage to the Tesla, separating the front of the car from the rear and breaching the high-voltage battery, which subsequently ignited in a post-crash fire. Following the initial collision, the Tesla was involved in additional impacts with nearby vehicles, further escalating the severity of the crash (National Transportation Safety Board, 2020).

The driver, who tragically died from the crash, was found to have been distracted, likely by a game on his smartphone. He did not intervene when Tesla's Autopilot system failed to detect and avoid the crash, leading to a preventable accident. In 2024, Tesla settled a wrongful death lawsuit with the driver's family. The settlement allowed Tesla to avoid airing evidence and testimonies in a widely-followed case (CNBC, 2024).

Why It Went Wrong:

There were two critical areas of failure in the 2018 Tesla crash: the technological limitations of the Autopilot system and the driver's overreliance on it. The Autopilot, intended to assist in lane-keeping, failed to maintain the vehicle's proper course and veered into the gore area without providing any alerts. Additionally, the vehicle's collision avoidance system was unable to detect the crash attenuator or trigger emergency braking, as the system was not equipped to recognize certain obstacles, particularly at high speeds. These failures highlight significant technological limitations in the system's ability to manage complex driving scenarios (National Transportation Safety Board, 2020).

On the human side, the driver's overreliance on the Autopilot system further exacerbated the issue. The driver, distracted by a smartphone game, did not intervene when the vehicle left its lane. Tesla's system did not effectively monitor the driver's engagement, allowing him to become fully disengaged from the driving task. This reliance on the system created a false sense of security, where the driver trusted the technology to handle complex driving situations that it was not designed for. As a result, no corrective actions were taken when the system failed, leading to the fatal crash (National Transportation Safety Board, 2020). This incident underscores the risks of using semi-autonomous systems without ensuring active human oversight, revealing a dangerous gap between the system's capabilities and the human expectation of full automation.

Lessons Learned:

Similar to the Uber case just discussed, the Tesla Autopilot crash emphasizes the critical need for continuous driver engagement, even when using advanced semi-autonomous systems. Drivers must be fully aware that these technologies are assistive, not fully autonomous, and overreliance on them can lead to catastrophic failures. This underscores the importance of educating users on the limitations of AI systems and ensuring they understand their responsibility to intervene when necessary.

Additionally, the case highlights the need for robust driver monitoring systems that keep drivers attentive, as well as fail-safe mechanisms that can activate in situations where AI systems misjudge or encounter complex scenarios. Features like emergency braking should serve as a protective layer, stepping in when both human and AI elements fail to respond appropriately. Ultimately, this incident shows that the balance between AI capabilities and human oversight is essential for ensuring safety in real-world, dynamic environments.

Advice for Balancing AI with Human Oversight

The failures discussed in this chapter illustrate the dangers of over-reliance on AI systems without adequate human oversight. To prevent similar issues in the future, the following best practices should be implemented:

1. Ensure Human Oversight: AI systems, particularly those that operate in safety-critical industries, must be designed to complement human judgment, not replace it. Human operators should remain engaged and have the ability to intervene when necessary.

2. Implement Fail-Safe Mechanisms: AI systems should be equipped with fail-safe mechanisms that allow humans to easily override the system in case of emergency. In high-risk environments like aviation or autonomous driving, these systems must prioritize human control in situations where the AI is uncertain or malfunctioning.

3. Comprehensive Training for Operators: Human operators must be trained not only in how to use AI systems but also in understanding the limitations of those systems. This includes recognizing when the AI is failing, behaving unpredictably, or approaching scenarios beyond its capabilities. Training should include clear guidelines on when and how to take control from the AI, ensuring that operators can step in effectively when the system's limitations are reached.

4. Test AI Systems in Real-World Conditions: AI systems should be rigorously tested in diverse, real-world conditions before being deployed. This helps ensure that the systems can handle the complexities and unpredictability of real-life scenarios.

5. Promote Transparent AI Design and Accountability: AI systems should be designed with transparency, enabling operators and stakeholders to understand how decisions are made. This also ensures accountability, providing clear documentation and mechanisms to trace back decisions to their source, allowing for better oversight and correction when things go wrong.

Conclusion: The Dangers of Blind Trust in AI

The case studies discussed in this chapter underscore a crucial reality; While artificial intelligence has revolutionized industries and delivered impressive efficiencies, it remains far from flawless. Over-reliance on AI systems, especially in high-stakes environments, poses significant risks when human oversight is reduced or removed entirely. From the tragic Boeing 737 MAX crashes to the Uber self-driving fatality and Tesla's Autopilot crash, these incidents highlight the devastating consequences of trusting automated systems to function without proper human intervention and fail-safe mechanisms.

AI's potential to streamline processes and improve decision-making is undeniable, but it cannot replace the nuanced, contextual judgment that human operators provide. Blind trust in AI systems, whether in aviation, autonomous driving, or other safety-critical sectors, can lead to catastrophic failures when the systems encounter unexpected scenarios or malfunction. The lesson here is that automation should always be seen as a support tool, augmenting human decision-making rather than replacing it entirely. Moreover, human operators must be equipped with the necessary training, authority, and tools to intervene when needed.

To prevent similar failures in the future, it is essential to maintain a balanced approach to AI implementation, where human oversight remains at the forefront. Organizations must ensure that their AI systems are robustly tested in real-world conditions, designed with multiple layers of fail-safes, and supported by human operators who are fully aware of both the system's capabilities and its limitations. This hybrid approach, where AI and human expertise work together, is crucial for mitigating risks and ensuring the safe, effective deployment of AI in high-risk industries.

Looking Ahead: Ethical and Legal Failures in AI

In the next chapter, we will delve into the ethical and legal implications of AI systems. While AI offers significant opportunities for innovation, it also raises complex ethical questions about privacy, accountability, and the potential for abuse. We will explore cases where AI has crossed ethical and legal boundaries.

Chapter 7: Ethical and Legal Failures in AI

As artificial intelligence (AI) continues to permeate various sectors of society, it offers tremendous opportunities for innovation and growth. From healthcare and finance to law enforcement and military operations, AI's potential to optimize processes and improve decision-making is unparalleled. However, with this potential comes a host of ethical and legal challenges that, if unaddressed, can lead to significant harm to individuals and society at large.

AI operates by analyzing vast amounts of data and identifying patterns that humans might miss. But when those patterns are derived from biased, incomplete, or unethical data sources, AI systems can replicate and amplify injustices rather than mitigate them. This risk is particularly pronounced in sensitive fields such as criminal justice, surveillance, and warfare, where AI can make decisions that affect people's lives, freedoms, and safety.

Moreover, the rapid development of AI has outpaced the evolution of legal frameworks. Governments and regulatory bodies are struggling to keep up with the ethical dilemmas posed by AI, creating a situation where harmful technologies can be deployed with little oversight or accountability. In some cases, AI systems have led to biased decision-making or even autonomous acts of violence. Without clear ethical guidelines and legal safeguards, the unchecked use of AI can result in dangerous and even disastrous outcomes.

In this chapter, we explore cases where the lack of clear ethical standards and legal frameworks led to significant AI failures. From biased algorithms in criminal justice to autonomous drones operating without human oversight, these case studies illustrate the urgent need for ethical and legal governance in AI development.

Case Study 1: COMPAS and Racial Bias in Criminal Justice

What Went Wrong:

COMPAS (Correctional Offender Management Profiling for Alternative Sanctions) is an algorithmic tool widely used in the U.S. criminal justice system to assess the likelihood of a defendant reoffending. It was designed to assist judges in making more objective decisions regarding bail, sentencing, and parole by providing a risk score. The intention was to use data to eliminate human bias and deliver fairer outcomes in the criminal justice system. However, in 2016, an investigative report by ProPublica revealed that COMPAS exhibited significant racial bias (ProPublica, 2016).

The analysis showed that the algorithm disproportionately gave Black defendants higher risk scores than white defendants, even when their criminal histories were similar. For example, Black defendants were nearly twice as likely to be falsely labeled as high-risk, while white defendants were more likely to be mislabeled as low risk (ProPublica, 2016). A 2018 study which assessed the accuracy, fairness, and limits of predicting recidivism found the COMPAS algorithm no more accurate or fair than predictions made by people with little or no criminal justice expertise (Dressel and Farid, 2018).

The use of algorithms like COMPAS in decision-making processes sparked concerns about fairness and accountability. Critics worry that these systems, often seen as objective, can perpetuate existing biases if trained on biased data. Moreover, because algorithms are treated as authoritative, there is a risk of over-reliance on their outputs, even when their accuracy and fairness are in question. This raises ethical concerns about transparency, as the proprietary nature of these tools limits the ability to fully assess and challenge their decisions.

Why It Went Wrong:

COMPAS, like many AI-driven tools, relies heavily on large datasets to train its algorithms and make predictions. However, much of the data used in recidivism risk assessments comes from historical periods marred by systemic issues such as mass incarceration, biased policing, and discriminatory bail and sentencing practices. These biases are deeply embedded in the data itself, which means that, when applied to modern AI systems like COMPAS, they may perpetuate the same racial disparities that the tool was intended to avoid. The outcome is that Black defendants are often unfairly labeled as high-risk more frequently than white defendants, even when their criminal histories are comparable, exacerbating racial inequities in the criminal justice system (Slaw, 2020).

Further compounding the issue, a 2018 study revealed that despite COMPAS using 137 variables in its risk assessment calculations, a simpler model using only two factors age and total number of prior convictions performed just as well in predicting recidivism (Dressel and Farid, 2018). This raises serious questions about the true value of the algorithm's complexity. Especially when COMPAS was found to be no more accurate or fair than people with little to no criminal justice experience as mentioned above (Dressel and Farid, 2018). The proprietary nature of such tools makes them a "black box" system, meaning their internal decision-making processes are hidden from judges, defendants, and the public (Duke Today, 2017). This lack of transparency not only makes it nearly impossible to scrutinize or challenge the algorithm's decisions but also leaves the legal system unable to correct potential biases in such tools. As a result, the courts may unknowingly rely on flawed, biased algorithms that disproportionately harm minority groups, reinforcing the very biases the system was supposed to counteract.

This situation highlights the need for greater transparency and accountability in AI-driven systems, especially those with such high stakes as criminal justice decisions. Without clear insight into how these algorithms operate and the biases they may reinforce, the promise of fairer, more objective decision-making remains unfulfilled, and the risks of perpetuating injustice are magnified.

Lessons Learned:

The COMPAS case underscores the critical importance of auditing AI systems for bias, especially in high-stakes environments like criminal justice, where decisions have life-altering consequences. Without proper oversight, algorithms can unintentionally perpetuate historical biases embedded in their training data, leading to unfair outcomes for marginalized communities. To combat this, AI systems must be regularly audited and updated to ensure fairness and accountability.

This case highlights the need for greater transparency and explainability in algorithmic decision-making. AI systems should not function as "black boxes" where their inner workings are hidden from users and stakeholders. Clear insight into how decisions are made allows for scrutiny and the ability to challenge potentially unjust outcomes. Without this transparency, the promise of fairer, more objective decision-making remains unfulfilled, and the risks of perpetuating injustice are magnified.

Moreover, this case illustrates that complexity does not guarantee accuracy or fairness in AI systems. Simpler models may often perform just as well or even better when it comes to ensuring fairness, without the opacity of more complex, proprietary algorithms. Developers and decision-makers must avoid over-reliance on opaque systems and instead prioritize rigorous testing for fairness, especially when these algorithms affect historically marginalized groups. By addressing these issues, we can work toward developing AI tools that contribute to more equitable and just outcomes.

Case Study 2: Autonomous Weapons and the Ethics of AI in Warfare

What Went Wrong:

In 2020, a UN report suggested that an autonomous drone may have attacked human targets in Libya without direct human oversight. The drone, known as the Kargu-2, was equipped with AI capable of tracking and engaging targets independently. While it's not entirely clear whether the drone acted fully autonomously, this incident is considered one of the earliest documented cases of autonomous weapons possibly carrying out lethal operations. This raised serious ethical concerns about the use of AI in warfare and the implications of allowing machines to make critical, life-or-death decisions (The New York Times, 2021).

The STM Kargu-2 drone, had the capability to operate autonomously, meaning it could make decisions about which targets to engage without direct human intervention. While it is not fully confirmed that the strike on retreating Libyan forces was conducted by an autonomous drone, these weapons systems were programmed with a "fire, forget, and find" capability, allowing them to potentially attack targets independently (United Nations Security Council, 2021). This raises significant concerns about accountability in warfare. If an AI system makes the wrong decision, such as harming civilians or violating international law, who is held responsible? The use of AI in lethal autonomous weapons presents a unique challenge by removing human judgment from situations requiring ethical and moral decision-making, which increases the risk of unintended consequences.

Why It Went Wrong:

The core ethical failure of the Kargu-2 drone lies in the delegation of lethal decision-making to an AI system. Machines lack the ability to make nuanced ethical judgments that are essential in combat situations, such as determining proportionality, identifying non-combatants, or assessing the necessity of lethal force (The New York Times, 2021). International humanitarian law is based on principles like the distinction between combatants and civilians, and the use of proportional force rules that an autonomous AI may not fully comprehend or apply.

The lack of human oversight in lethal decision-making, strips away the essential human judgment needed in complex combat scenarios. Autonomous systems like the Kargu-2 cannot assess intentions, differentiate between combatants and civilians, or apply proportional force with the nuance required by international humanitarian law. In response to these concerns, several countries and human rights organizations have called for an outright ban on fully autonomous "killer robots" (Human Rights Watch, 2020).

Lessons Learned:

The deployment of autonomous weapons in Libya demonstrates the urgent need for international regulations governing the use of AI in warfare. Human oversight should remain a key principle in any decision-making process that involves the use of lethal force. Nations must work together to develop clear legal and ethical boundaries for the use of autonomous systems in combat, ensuring that AI is used as a tool to assist human judgment rather than replace it. Furthermore, accountability mechanisms must be established to address the question of responsibility in cases where AI systems make lethal decisions.

Case Study 3: Microsoft Tay Chatbot — Unchecked AI in the Public Domain

What Went Wrong:

In 2016, Microsoft launched an AI-powered chatbot named Tay on Twitter, designed to engage in conversations and learn from user interactions. Tay was programmed to evolve based on the content it was exposed to, and the idea was that the more it interacted with people, the more natural and intelligent its responses would become. However, within hours of its launch, Tay began tweeting offensive, racist, and misogynistic comments due to the harmful language it absorbed from Twitter users (The Guardian, 2016).

Tay was quickly taken offline, but the damage was done. The chatbot, which was meant to showcase the potential of conversational AI, instead became an example of how easily AI can be corrupted when exposed to unregulated, real-time data. It also highlighted the risks of deploying AI systems in public environments without sufficient safeguards to prevent them from learning and replicating harmful behavior. Microsoft issued an apology admitting the experiment had gone badly wrong. It said it would revive Tay only if its engineers could find a way to prevent Web users from influencing the chatbot in ways that undermine the company's principles and values (The Guardian, 2016).

Why It Went Wrong:

Microsoft attributed Tay's failure to a coordinated attack by a group of users who exploited a vulnerability in the chatbot's design. While they had implemented various filters and stress-tested Tay under different conditions, they did not foresee this specific type of attack, where users taught Tay to tweet offensive and inappropriate content. Microsoft acknowledged that while they prepared for some forms of abuse, they overlooked the possibility of this type of malicious exploitation (Microsoft, 2016).

The failure of Microsoft's Tay chatbot can be attributed to its reliance on unsupervised learning from user interactions. After Tay's failure, various experts shared their thoughts on the underlying causes. Roman Yampolskiy head of the CyberSecurity lab at the University of Louisville, emphasized that "one needs to explicitly teach a system about what is not appropriate, like we do with children," underscoring the need for clear guidance to prevent harmful behavior. Louis Rosenberg the founder of Unanimous AI, highlighted that Tay, like other chatbots, mimicked inputs without understanding the meaning, comparing it to a parrot repeating bad language (Reese, 2016).

The filters in place were not sufficient to prevent Tay from learning inappropriate language or to guide its responses toward ethical or responsible behavior. The lack of adequate real-time monitoring and intervention further allowed Tay to spiral out of control before Microsoft could shut it down. This incident illustrated the importance of building robust ethical safeguards into AI systems, especially when they are deployed in public-facing environments where they can be influenced by unpredictable or malicious actors.

Lessons Learned:

The Microsoft Tay case illustrates the vital importance of ethical safeguards and continuous human oversight when deploying AI systems, particularly in public and interactive environments. AI systems must be designed with built-in protections that prevent them from learning harmful behaviors or amplifying toxic content, as Tay's exposure to unfiltered user interactions led it to adopt offensive language. This case shows that real-time monitoring and immediate intervention are crucial, ensuring that developers can respond quickly to unexpected or inappropriate behaviors.

Additionally, developers must anticipate potential misuse and ensure that AI systems are tested rigorously to identify vulnerabilities. Tay's failure demonstrates the dangers of relying on unsupervised learning in environments where users can manipulate the system's responses. Stronger safeguards and ethical guidelines are necessary to ensure that AI systems can operate safely without being influenced by malicious actors.

Finally, this case highlights the importance of programming AI systems with clear ethical boundaries to prevent them from reflecting the worst aspects of human input. Without these boundaries, AI systems are vulnerable to exploitation, as seen with Tay. By combining ethical governance, proactive safeguards, and human oversight, developers can ensure AI systems are better aligned with societal values and operate responsibly in real-world settings.

Advice for Preventing Ethical and Legal Failures in AI

As AI continues to play an increasingly prominent role across industries, it is crucial to ensure that systems are built and deployed in ways that protect individual rights and avoid unintended harm. Here are several key strategies to help mitigate the risks of ethical and legal failures in AI:

1. **Establish Clear Ethical Guidelines**: Companies and governments must develop and adhere to clear ethical frameworks that define the appropriate use of AI technologies. These frameworks should prioritize transparency, fairness, and accountability in how AI systems are designed, tested, and deployed. Involve interdisciplinary teams in the creation of these guidelines, including ethicists, legal experts, and representatives from affected communities, to ensure a well-rounded approach to governance.

2. Audit AI Systems for Bias: Regular audits should be conducted to assess AI systems for biases that could lead to discriminatory outcomes, particularly in areas such as criminal justice, hiring, and law enforcement. These audits should be performed both before and after deployment to ensure that the AI system evolves in a fair and ethical manner over time.

3. Implement Human Oversight: While AI systems can automate complex processes, human oversight remains essential, especially when decisions affect fundamental human rights, safety, or freedoms. Establish protocols that ensure AI systems are subject to human review before making high-stakes decisions, such as in law enforcement, healthcare, or military operations.

4. Enhance Transparency and Explainability: AI systems, particularly those that impact legal or ethical outcomes, must be transparent and explainable. Developers should design AI models that can provide clear reasoning for their decisions, allowing users to understand and challenge those decisions if necessary. Black-box AI models, which provide no insight into their decision-making processes, should be avoided in sensitive applications.

5. Advocate for Global AI Regulations: Policymakers and international bodies should work together to create unified regulations that govern the ethical deployment of AI, particularly in areas like autonomous weapons, surveillance, and law enforcement. An international framework will help prevent the proliferation of AI systems that operate without adequate legal or ethical oversight, thereby reducing the risk of harm on a global scale.

6. Incorporate Continuous Monitoring and Feedback: AI systems should be regularly monitored and updated based on real-world performance and user feedback. Continuous monitoring ensures that any ethical or legal issues that arise post-deployment can be addressed quickly and effectively. Developers should also allow for regular recalibration of AI models to account for shifts in societal norms, data patterns, and user behavior over time.

Conclusion: The Need for Ethical AI Governance

The case studies explored in this chapter illustrate the significant risks associated with AI when ethical and legal frameworks are absent. From the racial bias in COMPAS algorithms to the ethical implications of autonomous warfare with the Kargu-2 drone, the potential for AI to cause harm is undeniable. These examples highlight a critical juncture where the promise of innovation must be weighed against the risk of misuse and injustice.

As AI continues to evolve and integrate into society, robust governance, transparency, and accountability are essential. Stakeholders including governments, regulatory bodies, industry leaders, and the public must collaborate to establish comprehensive ethical guidelines that govern AI development and deployment. These frameworks should encompass diverse perspectives to ensure inclusivity and adaptability.

Clear legal regulations are necessary to oversee AI use in sensitive areas such as criminal justice and healthcare, addressing current and future ethical challenges. Regular audits of AI systems for bias and fairness must become standard practice, alongside fostering transparency and explainability to empower users to understand and challenge algorithmic decisions.

International cooperation is also vital in creating unified regulations for AI deployment. By advocating for ethical governance on a global scale, we can ensure that AI technologies uphold human rights and promote social justice.

While the challenges posed by AI are significant, so are the opportunities for transformative impact when these technologies are applied responsibly. By addressing the ethical and legal failures highlighted in this chapter, we can harness AI's potential as a tool for empowerment, striving for a future where technology enhances the human experience and fosters a more equitable society.

Looking Ahead: Privacy Failures in AI

As we've seen in the previous chapter, ethical and legal failures in AI can lead to significant societal harm, from biased criminal justice outcomes to uncontrolled autonomous systems. However, one of the most pervasive and far-reaching concerns is the threat to individual privacy posed by AI-driven technologies. With data collection at the core of AI's functionality, privacy violations have the potential to erode public trust, disrupt democratic processes, and cause widespread social unrest. In the next chapter, we will delve deeper into the privacy risks associated with AI systems, examining high-profile cases where the misuse of personal data led to severe breaches of privacy.

Chapter 8: Privacy Failures in AI

As AI systems continue to evolve, their ever-growing reliance on massive datasets raises urgent concerns about privacy in the digital age. From social media data mining and targeted advertising to large-scale surveillance, AI technologies have the potential to significantly infringe on individuals' privacy rights. These systems, often operating behind complex algorithms, can collect and process vast amounts of personal data, often without the clear knowledge or consent of users. This raises critical questions: how is this data being used, who has access to it, and to what extent are individuals' privacy rights being protected?

The consequences of privacy breaches in AI can be profound, affecting not only individual freedoms but also broader societal structures. When AI systems are used for surveillance or data profiling, they can inadvertently or intentionally influence behavior, curtail free expression, or contribute to social inequality. Furthermore, the erosion of privacy can result in a loss of public trust in both the technologies and the institutions that deploy them. High-profile cases like the Clearview AI scandal and the Facebook-Cambridge Analytica incident have made it clear that when privacy is compromised, the ripple effects can extend into politics, civil liberties, and democratic processes.

In this chapter, we explore several critical cases where AI-driven systems have led to major privacy violations, illustrating the tangible impact of these breaches on individuals and society. Through these case studies, we underscore the importance of building robust data protection frameworks and privacy regulations to govern the rapidly evolving landscape of AI. As the power and reach of AI systems continue to expand, the need for transparency, accountability, and ethical use of data has never been more crucial.

Case Study 1: Clearview AI and the Threat to Privacy

What Went Wrong:

In 2020, Clearview AI, a company specializing in facial recognition technology, came under intense scrutiny when it was revealed that they had scraped billions of photos from social media platforms like Facebook, YouTube, and Venmo without user consent. Clearview AI used these photos to build a database that could be accessed by law enforcement agencies, private companies, and even individuals. By simply uploading a photo, users could search for matches in the database, enabling them to identify and track people based on their online presence. This essentially created a tool for mass surveillance (The New York Times, 2020).

The controversy erupted when privacy advocates revealed that Clearview AI had collected and used personal images without the knowledge or consent of the individuals in those photos. It was also discovered that law enforcement agencies were using the tool to identify suspects, raising concerns about civil liberties and the potential for abuse (The Register, 2021). Not only were there concerns about the ethical implications of such a powerful surveillance tool, but there were also fears about how easily this technology could fall into the wrong hands.

Why It Went Wrong:

Clearview AI's failure was rooted in its blatant disregard for privacy and consent. The company built its business model on scraping publicly available data, assuming that since the images were on social media platforms, they were fair game. This violates basic principles of data privacy and ethics. Clearview did not obtain permission from the individuals whose photos were used, nor did it offer them any recourse to opt out of the database. This lack of transparency and accountability make Clearview AI's actions not only ethically questionable but also legally dubious.

Australia took a strong stance against Clearview's collection of facial images of its citizens. The Office of the Australian Information Commissioner (OAIC) ruled on 14 October 2021 that Clearview AI had violated the Privacy Act by collecting facial images without consent. Although the company appealed, it withdrew its case in August 2023 before the tribunal could issue a ruling, leaving the original decision in place. Clearview AI was required to cease collecting images from Australians and delete all previously collected data (Office of the Australian Information Commissioner, 2021).

The absence of comprehensive federal data privacy regulations in the United States enabled Clearview AI to operate in a legal gray area. Unlike the European Union, with its strict General Data Protection Regulation (GDPR), the U.S. relies on a patchwork of state-level laws, creating inconsistent oversight. While some states, like California, have enacted stronger privacy laws, such as the California Privacy Rights Act (CPRA), the lack of a unified national framework allowed Clearview AI to exploit gaps in accountability and regulation.

Lessons Learned:

The Clearview AI case serves as a cautionary tale about the dangers of unchecked surveillance technology and underscores the urgent need for stricter data privacy laws. It highlights the critical importance of obtaining informed consent from individuals before utilizing their personal data. Companies must ensure that users are fully aware of how their data will be collected, used, and shared, fostering a culture of transparency that builds trust with the public.

Moreover, the case emphasizes the necessity for governments and regulatory bodies to establish clearer guidelines governing the collection and use of personal data, particularly in surveillance and law enforcement contexts. These guidelines should prioritize user privacy and civil liberties, ensuring that individuals are protected from potential abuses of powerful AI tools. The absence of comprehensive federal data privacy regulations in the United States creates a patchwork of state-level laws that can be exploited, making it imperative to develop a unified national framework that provides consistent oversight and protection for personal data.

Additionally, companies must prioritize accountability in their data practices, providing clear information about how data is used and allowing individuals the option to opt out of data collection when desired. As surveillance technologies advance, stakeholders must remain vigilant about the potential for misuse, implementing robust safeguards and accountability mechanisms to prevent the exploitation of these powerful tools.

Case Study 2: Facebook and the Cambridge Analytica Scandal

What Went Wrong:

The Facebook-Cambridge Analytica scandal is one of the most infamous examples of data privacy violations. In 2018, it was revealed that Cambridge Analytica, a political consulting firm, had harvested the personal data of up to eighty-seven million Facebook users without their consent (BBC News, 2022). The data was allegedly then used to create detailed voter profiles and deliver targeted political ads during the 2016 U.S. presidential election and the Brexit referendum (The Guardian, 2018c). This raised serious concerns about data privacy, manipulation, and the role of AI in influencing democratic processes.

Cambridge Analytica gained access to the data through a third-party app that collected information not only from users who consented to participate but also from their friends' profiles (CNBC, 2018). The company then is reported to have used AI algorithms to analyze the data and create psychographic profiles, which helped them target specific groups of voters with tailored political messaging (Politico, 2020). Facebook was criticized for its lax data privacy policies, which allowed such widespread data harvesting to occur unnoticed.

The fallout from the Cambridge Analytica scandal was significant for both Facebook and Cambridge Analytica. In 2019, the U.S. Federal Trade Commission (FTC) imposed a record $5 billion fine on Facebook for its role in the data breach and its failure to protect user privacy. This was the largest fine ever imposed by the FTC, highlighting the severity of Facebook's privacy violations (Reuters, 2019). While Facebook faced public backlash and multiple regulatory investigations, the #DeleteFacebook movement also gained traction, with users becoming increasingly concerned about how their personal data was mishandled (CBS News, 2018).

Likewise, Cambridge Analytica faced drastic consequences. Following the revelations of their misuse of Facebook data to influence political campaigns, the company became the subject of intense scrutiny. Multiple investigations were launched, including inquiries by the British Information Commissioner's Office and the U.S. Congress. Under mounting pressure, Cambridge Analytica shut down in May 2018, citing a loss of business and reputational damage. The company and its parent organization, SCL Group, filed for bankruptcy and ceased operations, marking the end of its involvement in political consulting (The Guardian, 2018c).

Why It Went Wrong:

The root of the problem lay in Facebook’s data-sharing policies and lack of oversight over third-party apps. Cambridge Analytica, through the app thisisyourdigitallife, collected data not only from users who took the app’s survey but also from their Facebook friends, without explicit permission from those friends (The Guardian, 2018d). This enabled Cambridge Analytica to harvest personal information from more than eighty-seven million Facebook users (BBC News, 2022).

While Facebook's platform policies technically allowed apps to collect friends' data to enhance user experience, it explicitly prohibited the sale or use of this data for advertising or commercial purposes. Cambridge Analytica violated this rule by using the data to create detailed profiles of U.S. voters, which were then allegedly used to craft targeted political advertisements designed to influence voter behavior in the 2016 U.S. presidential election (The Guardian, 2018d).

Despite discovering the data misuse by late 2015, Facebook failed to notify users or take strong action. Instead, Facebook only asked Cambridge Analytica to certify that the data had been deleted. This delayed response and failure to act swiftly worsened the situation, leaving millions of users vulnerable to data exploitation and manipulation (The Guardian, 2018d).

These revelations, brought to light by whistleblower Christopher Wylie, led to widespread public outrage and regulatory investigations in both the U.S. and UK into the use of data analytics for political purposes. Facebook's inadequate response to the misuse of data raised significant concerns about accountability and transparency in the handling of personal information (The Guardian, 2018d).

Additionally, the likely use of AI in processing and analyzing the vast amount of data harvested from Facebook users allowed Cambridge Analytica to influence public opinion on an unprecedented scale. By leveraging AI-driven profiling, Cambridge Analytica was able to sort through millions of data points and create detailed profiles of voters' personalities, preferences, and psychological traits. This enabled the company to craft hyper-targeted political ads designed to resonate with specific emotional triggers and personal concerns of individual voters (Politico, 2020).

The AI algorithms played a crucial role in processing the data and predicting which users were most susceptible to specific messaging (Politico, 2020). By tailoring political ads to exploit voters' perceived vulnerabilities, Cambridge Analytica's AI-driven strategies likely influenced voter behavior in highly targeted ways. This raised significant ethical concerns about the use of AI for political manipulation, as the combination of personal data, psychological insights, and AI predictions allowed for precise interventions in people's decision-making processes without their knowledge or consent.

These revelations highlighted the potential for AI to be used as a powerful tool in shaping political outcomes, raising questions about the ethical limits of such technology in democracy. The use of AI in this context not only violated privacy but also called into question the fairness of using automated systems to influence deeply personal and political decisions.

Lessons Learned:

The Facebook-Cambridge Analytica scandal underscores the urgent need for stronger data privacy regulations and greater oversight of how companies collect, manage, and share personal data. It highlights the critical importance of user consent and transparency in data collection practices, ensuring that individuals fully understand how their data is being used and retain control over its access and distribution. Platforms like Facebook must be held accountable not only for their own data practices but also for the actions of third parties that access and use user data through their systems.

This case also demonstrates the ethical risks of AI-driven data analysis, as Cambridge Analytica's psychographic profiling exploited users' personal data to influence voter behavior in ways that were not fully understood or consented to. The scandal illustrates the potential for AI systems to be used for political manipulation, raising concerns about the fairness and ethical use of such technology in sensitive areas like democratic elections.

Additionally, the case highlights the necessity of accountability and swift action. Facebook's delayed response after discovering the misuse of data allowed the problem to escalate, resulting in legal and financial consequences, including a $5 billion fine by the FTC. To prevent future breaches, companies must prioritize user privacy, establish robust safeguards, and take immediate action when violations occur to maintain public trust and ensure that personal data is used ethically.

Advice for Preventing Privacy Failures in AI

1. **Obtain Explicit User Consent**: AI systems must be transparent about the data they collect and how they intend to use it. Companies should seek explicit consent from users, providing clear and easy-to-understand options for managing their privacy settings. It's important that users know exactly what data is being collected and have the option to opt out.

2. **Strengthen Data Privacy Regulations**: Governments should enforce stricter data privacy regulations, such as the General Data Protection Regulation (GDPR) and the California Consumer Privacy Act (CCPA), to ensure companies are held accountable for how they collect, store, and process personal data. Consistent audits and legal consequences for violations are crucial in protecting user data.

3. **Promote Transparency and Accountability**: AI companies must promote transparency in their data practices, ensuring users know what is being tracked and how the data is being used.

Clear documentation and reports about data use can help restore public trust in AI systems. Accountability frameworks, where companies are held responsible for privacy violations, should be adopted industry wide.

4. Invest in Data Security: Companies should prioritize data security measures to prevent unauthorized access to personal data. By implementing encryption, regular security audits, and breach detection systems, businesses can protect user data from malicious actors and safeguard against accidental breaches.

5. Implement Real-Time Monitoring: Companies should monitor their AI systems in real-time to identify any potential misuse of data or unexpected behavior. Continuous monitoring and prompt intervention can help mitigate the impact of privacy breaches before they escalate.

Conclusion: Privacy as a Foundation for Trust in AI

The case studies discussed in this chapter illuminate the critical importance of privacy in AI-driven systems. Privacy breaches not only undermine public trust but also expose companies to significant regulatory and legal consequences. High-profile incidents, such as the Clearview AI scandal and the Facebook-Cambridge Analytica debacle, have underscored the profound risks associated with the misuse of personal data. When individuals' privacy rights are compromised, the repercussions extend far beyond personal inconvenience, they can threaten democratic processes, civil liberties, and societal stability.

As AI technologies continue to evolve and permeate various aspects of our lives, it is imperative that companies prioritize data protection and transparency as foundational principles of their operations. Building and maintaining user trust in AI systems necessitates a commitment to ethical data practices that respect individuals' rights. Stronger privacy regulations, such as those established by the General Data Protection Regulation (GDPR) and the California Consumer Privacy Act (CCPA), are essential in creating a robust legal framework to safeguard personal information.

Moreover, organizations must actively cultivate a culture of accountability where data practices are regularly audited, and violations are met with meaningful consequences. This commitment to transparency not only helps mitigate risks but also empowers users to make informed decisions about their personal data. By integrating privacy considerations into the design and implementation of AI systems, companies can foster an environment where innovation thrives alongside the protection of fundamental rights.

In this digital age, the necessity for ethical data management and respect for privacy has never been more crucial. By prioritizing privacy, we can ensure that AI serves as a tool for empowerment rather than oppression, ultimately leading to a more equitable and just society. The path forward requires collective efforts from businesses, governments, and individuals to establish a framework that not only harnesses the power of AI but also upholds the values of transparency, accountability, and respect for human dignity.

Looking Ahead: Financial Losses Due to AI Misjudgments

While privacy concerns are among the most visible challenges in AI today, financial misjudgments also present significant risks. In the next chapter, we will explore how AI systems, when improperly designed or misused, can lead to financial losses for businesses and individuals. Through real-world case studies, we'll analyze the economic risks posed by AI and how these risks can be mitigated.

Chapter 9: Financial Losses Due to AI Misjudgments

Artificial intelligence (AI) has rapidly become a key driver of business decision-making, automation, and operational efficiency across various industries. From financial trading and loan approvals to real estate valuations and inventory management, AI promises speed, precision, and profitability. However, when AI systems misfire, the financial impact can be catastrophic. This can happen when algorithms fail to account for changing market conditions, misinterpret data, or are deployed without sufficient human oversight.

In recent years, there have been several high-profile instances where AI misjudgments led to significant financial losses. These failures are often the result of over-reliance on AI-driven decision-making, insufficiently trained models, or a lack of continuous human monitoring. Whether in finance, retail, or real estate such as Zillow Offers as discussed earlier, these errors have proven costly, highlighting the importance of developing robust risk management protocols for AI.

In this chapter, we'll examine notable cases where AI misjudgments resulted in financial losses. Through these case studies, we'll explore the reasons behind the failures and provide key insights to prevent similar outcomes in the future.

Case Study 1: Air Canada's Chatbot Refund Error

What Went Wrong:

In early 2024, Air Canada faced a significant public relations issue when its AI-powered customer service chatbot incorrectly issued a refund for a non-refundable ticket. The chatbot, designed to streamline customer inquiries and handle tasks such as refund requests, mistakenly approved the refund without checking the customer's eligibility under the airline's strict refund policies When the customer attempted to claim the refund, Air Canada initially refused to honor it, citing that the ticket was non-refundable. However, the customer took legal action, and during the proceedings, Air Canada controversially argued that "the chatbot is a separate legal entity responsible for its own actions," attempting to deflect responsibility for the error onto the AI system (TechHQ, 2024).

This stance backfired, drawing public criticism as many viewed it as an attempt to avoid accountability for the actions of its AI system. Ultimately, Air Canada was forced to honor the refund, resulting in both a financial loss and damage to its reputation. While the immediate financial damage was not catastrophic, the incident raised concerns about the reliability of the AI system, particularly regarding its handling of complex customer transactions like refund requests. The error exposed potential weaknesses in the airline's reliance on AI for customer service, highlighting the need for better oversight and human intervention in complex cases.

Why It Went Wrong:

The failure likely stemmed from a combination of AI hallucinations, insufficient guardrails, inadequate fine-tuning, and insufficient real-world testing. The chatbot likely "hallucinated" the refund policy, providing inaccurate information about bereavement fares. This likely happened because the system lacked robust guardrails rules that ensure AI outputs align with company policies, allowing for off-policy responses that misled the customer (CMSWire, 2024). An article in the New York times, reported on research which found AI chatbots may hallucinate 3% to 27% of the time, leading to incorrect or misleading responses (The New York Times, 2023).

In addition the chatbot also may have suffered from inadequate fine-tuning. Without continuous adjustments based on real-world interactions, it failed to accurately handle complex refund queries. If tested rigorously in a variety of cases, including edge cases involving non-refundable tickets, this error may have been identified and corrected prior to deployment.

Lessons Learned:

The Air Canada chatbot failure reveals several key lessons for effectively deploying AI in customer service. One of the most important takeaways is the need for strong guardrails to ensure that AI responses align with company policies. In this case, clearer boundaries could have prevented the chatbot from providing inaccurate refund information, reducing the risk of costly errors.

Equally important is continuous fine-tuning of AI systems. Regularly updating the chatbot based on real-world customer interactions would have allowed it to better handle complex situations, such as determining eligibility for non-refundable ticket refunds. The incident also highlights the importance of rigorous real-world testing. Testing the AI in a variety of scenarios, including edge cases, could have helped identify the system's flaws before it was rolled out to customers.

Additionally, this case underscores the importance of understanding liability when using AI in customer interactions. The British Columbia Civil Resolution Tribunal ruled that Air Canada was responsible for all information provided on its website, including that generated by its chatbot (BBC News, 2024). This decision emphasizes that companies cannot absolve themselves of liability by blaming AI systems for errors.

Ensuring that AI is accurate and reliable is critical for protecting both the company and its customers from financial and legal repercussions.

Case Study 2: Knight Capital's $440 Million Trading Loss

What Went Wrong:

On August 1, 2012, Knight Capital's automated trading system malfunctioned during the deployment of new software intended for the New York Stock Exchange's Retail Liquidity Program. One of Knight's servers still contained outdated code, which mistakenly triggered high-volume trading activity. Over a 45-minute period, the system sent millions of erroneous trade orders to the market. This led to Knight unintentionally buying $3.5 billion in stocks and selling $3.15 billion short, causing massive price fluctuations across 154 stocks. By the time the issue was resolved, Knight had incurred a loss of $460 million (U.S. Securities and Exchange Commission, 2013).

Knight Capital's reliance on automated trading systems, without sufficient testing and safeguards, led to the firm's near collapse.

Why It Went Wrong:

The failure occurred due to several interrelated factors. Firstly, Knight Capital's inadequate risk management controls played a critical role. The new software was not properly deployed on one of the servers, leaving the outdated "Power Peg" code active, which was inadvertently triggered and led to uncontrolled trade executions. Knight's lack of testing and safeguards exacerbated the issue, as the deployment was not reviewed by a second technician, and the system was not thoroughly tested. Additionally, Knight lacked sufficient controls to prevent erroneous orders from exceeding capital thresholds, as required under regulatory rules.

Further compounding the issue, Knight failed to establish and document adequate risk management controls as required by regulatory rules, including a comprehensive written description of their risk procedures. The company also lacked appropriate technology, governance, and oversight during the deployment of the code, allowing the old code to remain active without proper testing. These failures collectively led to a market disruption and a significant financial loss (U.S. Securities and Exchange Commission, 2013).

The incident highlights the risks of deploying new code without thorough testing, the absence of clear incident response procedures, and the failure to implement strong governance and supervisory protocols for technology management.

Lessons Learned:

The Knight Capital incident underscores the critical importance of rigorous testing and continuous monitoring of trading systems. High-frequency trading environments leave little room for error; even small mistakes can quickly escalate into significant financial losses. To prevent such disasters, companies must implement comprehensive testing protocols before deploying new software, ensuring that all systems are functioning correctly and that any outdated code is eliminated.

Moreover, maintaining real-time monitoring is essential to catch potential issues early. Companies should establish robust risk management protocols that include fail-safe mechanisms capable of halting trading operations in the event of a malfunction. This proactive approach can prevent errors from escalating into catastrophic events, protecting both the firm and the broader market from disruptive consequences.

Additionally, the importance of thorough documentation and oversight cannot be overstated. Clear incident response procedures and strong governance structures are vital for effective technology management. By prioritizing these elements, firms can create a resilient framework that safeguards against the risks associated with automated trading systems.

Advice for Preventing Financial Losses Due to AI Misjudgments

AI offers powerful capabilities in financial decision-making, but it is crucial that businesses implement the right safeguards to mitigate the risks of costly errors. The following best practices can help prevent AI misjudgments from leading to major financial losses:

1. **Combine AI with Human Oversight**: AI should augment human decision-making, not replace it. In high-risk industries like finance, human experts are essential for validating AI-driven decisions and stepping in when the system fails to account for unexpected changes in the market.

2. **Thorough Testing and Monitoring**: Before deploying AI systems, companies must conduct rigorous testing in a variety of real-world scenarios. Continuous monitoring during live operations ensures that any malfunction or misjudgment can be quickly detected and corrected.

3. **Use Diverse and Up-to-Date Data**: AI models should be trained on high-quality, diverse datasets that reflect both historical and current market conditions. Relying solely on past data can lead to misjudgments, particularly in volatile environments.

4. **Implement Fail-Safes and Risk Management Protocols**: Companies should put in place robust fail-safe mechanisms that can automatically halt or override AI systems when things go

wrong. Risk management protocols must be integrated into AI systems to minimize the impact of errors.

5. Regularly Recalibrate AI Models: AI systems should be regularly updated and recalibrated to ensure that they remain relevant and accurate in changing market environments. Continuous updates help AI adapt to new trends and reduce the risk of misjudgments.

Conclusion: Navigating the Risks of AI in Financial Decision-Making

The case studies presented in this chapter underscore the profound financial risks associated with over-reliance on AI systems. Whether it involves predicting house prices such as the Zillow Offers, executing high-stakes trades, or managing loan approvals, the effectiveness of AI is fundamentally tied to the quality of the data it is trained on and the safeguards implemented to monitor its performance. To avoid costly misjudgments, organizations must recognize AI as a powerful tool that complements and enhances human expertise, rather than replacing it.

As AI continues to reshape financial markets and business strategies, it is crucial for organizations to learn from past failures and establish robust controls to mitigate risks. This includes integrating human oversight into AI operations, conducting thorough testing, and ensuring that models are continually recalibrated to adapt to changing market conditions. By harnessing the strengths of both AI and human decision-making, companies can unlock the full potential of AI technologies while minimizing the associated risks. In doing so, they can foster a more resilient financial landscape, where innovation thrives alongside accountability and prudence.

Looking Ahead: AI in Healthcare — When Lives Are at Stake

In finance, AI failures can result in financial loss, but in healthcare, the stakes are even higher, human lives. In the next chapter, we will investigate how AI is transforming healthcare and the serious implications of its failures in medical decision-making. Through case studies of AI-driven misdiagnoses and treatment errors, we'll explore how to balance innovation with safety in healthcare AI systems.

Chapter 10: AI in Healthcare — When Lives Are at Stake

The integration of artificial intelligence (AI) into healthcare has opened the door to a new era of medical diagnostics, treatment planning, and personalized care. From AI-driven imaging systems that can detect tumors in their earliest stages to algorithms that help predict patient outcomes, the potential for AI to revolutionize healthcare is immense. By automating routine tasks, reducing human error, and processing vast datasets, AI promises to enhance precision and efficiency across the medical field.

However, the power of AI in healthcare is a double-edged sword. When AI systems function as intended, they can drastically improve patient outcomes, but when they fail, the consequences can be life-threatening. A misdiagnosis, a poorly suggested treatment plan, or an overlooked symptom could lead to delayed or incorrect treatments, risking patients' lives. Unlike other industries where AI failures result in financial or operational setbacks, in healthcare the stakes are much higher as AI mistakes can cost lives.

In this chapter, we explore case studies that illustrate some failures of AI in healthcare, shedding light on the inherent risks and underscoring the critical need for robust testing, diverse datasets, human oversight, and ethical safeguards when deploying AI systems in medical contexts.

Case Study 1: IBM Watson's Cancer Treatment Failure

What Went Wrong:

IBM Watson for Oncology was initially heralded as a groundbreaking tool, expected to transform cancer treatment by offering oncologists precise, data-driven recommendations. Watson's AI system was tasked with analyzing massive datasets, including medical literature, clinical trial results, and patient records, to suggest optimal treatment plans for cancer patients. However, in 2018, reports surfaced that Watson had been delivering incorrect and sometimes dangerous recommendations, including one instance where it recommended a treatment that could cause severe bleeding for a patient with lung cancer (Stat News, 2018).

Why It Went Wrong:

Watson's failure can likely be attributed to its limited training on real-world data. It was reported that instead of using actual patient cases, Watson for Oncology was primarily trained on synthetic cases created by doctors at Memorial Sloan Kettering Cancer Center. This restricted dataset did not capture the complexity and variability of real-world cancer scenarios, leading Watson to produce flawed and sometimes unsafe treatment recommendations. Internal documents revealed that Watson's recommendations were often based on the expertise of a small group of specialists rather than widely accepted guidelines, raising concerns about the accuracy and reliability of its advice (Stat News, 2018).

Additionally, the reported feedback from clinicians highlighted that Watson's suggestions were not always appropriate and, in some cases, contradicted national treatment guidelines. IBM's internal assessments confirmed that the training methods, including the use of synthetic cases, played a significant role in these issues, contributing to dissatisfaction among customers and a lack of trust in Watson's recommendations (Stat News, 2018).

Lessons Learned:

The failure of IBM Watson for Oncology underscores the critical importance of using comprehensive, real-world training data in healthcare AI systems. Relying primarily on synthetic cases can lead to flawed and potentially harmful recommendations, as evidenced by Watson's inaccurate treatment suggestions.

Transparency is essential for trust; clinicians must understand the rationale behind AI-generated recommendations to assess their appropriateness and ensure alignment with established medical guidelines. Human oversight remains vital, as AI should complement rather than replace the expertise of healthcare providers. Clinicians must verify AI outputs to tailor recommendations to individual patient needs.

Additionally, ongoing evaluation and feedback mechanisms are crucial. Regular performance assessments, coupled with clinician input, can help identify shortcomings and enhance the system's reliability over time. By prioritizing these principles robust training data, transparency, human oversight, and continuous evaluation, healthcare organizations can leverage AI effectively while minimizing associated risks.

Case Study 2: Lokken v. UnitedHealth Group et al. (Filed November 14, 2023)

What Went Wrong:

In a class-action lawsuit filed in November 2023, it is claimed that UnitedHealth Group, along with its subsidiaries UnitedHealthcare and naviHealth, wrongfully denied post-acute care to Medicare Advantage Plan members through its use of the *nH Predict* AI model. According to the complaint, the AI system frequently overruled the treating physicians' recommendations, prematurely discontinuing coverage for necessary care. Plaintiffs allege that the AI-driven denials had a significant error rate, with more than 90% of these decisions overturned upon appeal. This led to patients either paying for care out-of-pocket or being forced to leave care facilities early, resulting in both financial and health-related consequences for elderly and vulnerable patients (*The Estate of Gene B. Lokken et al. v. UnitedHealth Group, Inc. et al.*, 2023)

What Went Wrong:

The lawsuit argues that UnitedHealth's reliance on the *nH Predict* AI model to make coverage decisions was a primary factor in the wrongful denials. The AI system, which was intended to predict how long patients would need post-acute care, applied rigid criteria based on historical data, often failing to account for individual patient complexities and evolving medical conditions. Furthermore, the plaintiffs claim that UnitedHealth employees were pressured to adhere to the AI's predictions, limiting their ability to make exceptions based on real-time clinical assessments. The lack of transparency surrounding the proprietary AI system and its decision-making process further complicated matters, making it difficult for patients or physicians to challenge the algorithm's outcomes (The Estate of Gene B. Lokken et al. v. UnitedHealth Group, Inc. et al., 2023).

This Centers for Medicare & Medicaid Services (CMS) in a 2024 memo to Medicare Advantage insurers weighed in on the matter. CMS clarified that health care coverage decisions cannot be made solely based on algorithms or artificial intelligence. Specifically, CMS stated that insurers must "base the decision on the individual patient's circumstances," including their medical history, physician recommendations, and clinical notes. Using an AI model that makes decisions based on a large data set, rather than individual patient factors, would not be compliant with CMS rules. The memo outlined that AI tools may assist in predicting care needs, but those predictions alone cannot be used as the basis for terminating or denying services. Insurers must reassess each patient's condition and provide detailed explanations for any denials, ensuring that coverage decisions are personalized and based on applicable coverage criteria (Centers for Medicare & Medicaid Services, 2024). This clarification followed the above lawsuit.

Lessons Learned:

One of the key lessons learned from the UnitedHealth case involving the *nH Predict* AI model is that AI should be used to assist in healthcare decision-making, not to replace it. The lawsuit illustrates the dangers of allowing AI systems to make final decisions about patient care without sufficient human oversight. In this instance it is alleged, the AI overruled clinical judgments, leading to premature denials of necessary care. This highlights the importance of AI systems being used as support tools that augment the expertise of healthcare providers, allowing them to make more informed decisions rather than bypassing their judgment altogether.

Another crucial takeaway is the need for transparency in AI models. The proprietary nature of the *nH Predict* tool, as outlined in the lawsuit, allegedly made it difficult for patients and physicians to understand how decisions were being made or to challenge those decisions effectively.

Transparency is essential to ensure that AI models used in healthcare are open to scrutiny, allowing clinicians and patients to see how the algorithms are reaching their conclusions. This openness not only builds trust but also provides opportunities for external validation, ensuring that the models are functioning as intended.

Lastly, accuracy and adaptability are critical for AI systems in healthcare. The *nH Predict* model allegedly applied rigid, one-size-fits-all criteria based on historical data, which failed to account for the complexities of individual patients' evolving medical conditions. AI models must be flexible and capable of adjusting to real-time data and patient-specific circumstances. Failure to do so can lead to inaccurate predictions and inappropriate denials of care. This underscores the need for AI models to continuously evolve, be monitored and be trained on diverse data sets to ensure they are accurate and responsive to the nuances of patient care.

Case Study 3: Epic Systems' Predictive Health Tool Failures

What Went Wrong:

Epic Systems, one of the largest electronic health record (EHR) providers, developed an AI-powered tool designed to predict which hospitalized patients were at risk of developing sepsis, a potentially life-threatening condition. The aim was to aid healthcare providers in detecting sepsis early, offering them the ability to prioritize patients in need of urgent intervention. However, despite its promise, a 2021 study revealed significant issues with the tool's accuracy. The sepsis prediction model underperformed in real world testing compared to the results reported by its developers. The model often failed to identify patients at risk, missing critical cases of sepsis. Conversely, it also generated numerous false positives, which resulted in unnecessary treatments and interventions. These errors caused both delays in treating actual sepsis cases and increased burdens on clinical staff due to unwarranted alerts and interventions (Wong et al., 2021). This underperformance and the variability of the tool's predictions across different hospital environments further contributed to its clinical ineffectiveness.

Why It Went Wrong:

The Epic Sepsis Model (ESM) experienced notable performance issues in real-world clinical settings, which diverged from the initial performance claims made during its development. A possible contributor to this underperformance was the model's proprietary nature, which limited transparency and independent validation. The lack of publicly available data about its effectiveness made it difficult for researchers and clinicians to thoroughly evaluate the model before its deployment in hospitals. This "black box" issue is especially concerning because proprietary models like the ESM can see a decline in performance over time as they fail to adapt to changes in clinical environments or patient populations. Independent assessments revealed that the model's real-world accuracy was notably lower than what had been reported during development (Wong et al., 2021).

A 2023 study highlighted that a major flaw in the ESM was its tendency to predict sepsis after clinicians had already detected it and taken action. This delay in prediction undermined the model's purpose of supporting early intervention, rendering its output redundant in many cases. Studies showed that the model failed to provide real-time, actionable insights that could augment clinical decision-making, which was a key promise of the tool during its rollout (Schertz et al., 2023).

Additionally, the model's performance varied significantly across different hospitals, especially in settings with higher rates of sepsis or more complex patient populations, such as those with multiple comorbidities. In these environments, the ESM struggled to differentiate between sepsis and other conditions that share similar symptoms, reducing its predictive accuracy. Differences in how hospitals documented patient data further contributed to these inconsistencies. The model appeared to work better in lower-acuity hospitals where the patient population and sepsis incidence were less complex, suggesting that it may not be as robust in high-acuity or teaching hospitals (Lyons, Hofford, Yu, et al., 2023).

Efforts to address these shortcomings include planned updates to the ESM by its developers, which will involve training the model on hospital-specific data and refining its definition of sepsis onset. These improvements aim to reduce variability across different environments and enhance the model's ability to provide meaningful, real-time support to clinicians (Lyons, Hofford, Yu, et al., 2023).

Lessons Learned:

The challenges faced by the Epic Sepsis Model (ESM) highlight key lessons for AI deployment in healthcare. One of the most important factors is the need for transparency and independent validation. The model's proprietary nature limited access to critical performance data, preventing external evaluation and contributing to its underperformance in real-world settings. Without rigorous testing across diverse environments, claims made during development may fail to hold true in practice. AI models, particularly in healthcare, must undergo independent assessments to ensure they function effectively in varied clinical contexts.

Another crucial lesson is the importance of providing real-time, actionable insights. The ESM often predicted sepsis after clinicians had already taken action, negating the tool's purpose of early detection. For AI to enhance clinical decision-making, it must seamlessly integrate into workflows and provide timely information that clinicians cannot easily obtain on their own.

The model's variability across different hospitals underscores the need for adaptability. The ESM struggled in high-acuity environments with complex patients, revealing that AI tools must be tailored to specific hospital data and conditions. Additionally, continuous human oversight is essential to ensure that AI systems do not operate in isolation. Healthcare providers need to regularly monitor the tool's outputs and adjust its use based on real-world feedback. This human oversight, combined with ongoing updates and refinements to the AI stool, as seen in efforts to retrain the ESM, is crucial for maintaining its relevance and accuracy over time.

These lessons illustrate that while AI holds promise in healthcare, caution is needed when relying on developer claims. Proper validation, adaptability, human oversight, and ongoing updates are critical for ensuring these tools deliver meaningful improvements in patient care.

Advice for Safely Deploying AI in Healthcare

The failures discussed in this chapter underscore the critical need for safety, testing, and human oversight when deploying AI systems in healthcare. To mitigate the risks associated with AI misjudgments, the following best practices should be implemented:

1. **Train AI on Diverse and Comprehensive Datasets**: AI systems must be trained on data that reflects the diversity of real-world patient populations, including different age groups, ethnicities, geographic regions, and medical histories. This ensures the AI can generalize its predictions across diverse patient populations.

2. **Ensure Transparency and Explainability**: AI systems should be transparent and explainable. Clinicians need to understand the reasoning behind the AI's recommendations to

trust its conclusions. AI models must be able to provide justifications for their outputs so that healthcare professionals can assess their validity.

3. Conduct Rigorous Testing Across Multiple Clinical Settings: AI systems must be rigorously tested and validated in a variety of clinical environments to ensure they perform accurately in different settings. Real-world testing in diverse hospital systems is essential before deploying AI on a large scale.

4. Maintain Human Oversight in High-Stakes Decision-Making: AI systems should never replace the judgment of healthcare professionals. In life-or-death scenarios, human oversight is critical to ensuring that AI-generated recommendations are accurate and appropriate for the patient's specific condition.

5. Regularly Update AI Models with New Medical Data: Medical knowledge and best practices evolve rapidly. AI models should be continuously updated to reflect the latest research and clinical data, ensuring their recommendations remain accurate and aligned with current medical standards.

Conclusion: Balancing Innovation with Patient Safety

The integration of AI into healthcare stands at the intersection of immense promise and significant peril. AI's potential to revolutionize diagnostics, treatment planning, and patient care is undeniable, as it offers unparalleled speed, precision, and data-driven insights. However, as illustrated by the case studies in this chapter, the stakes are extraordinarily high when AI systems falter. A single error in a life-or-death situation can have devastating consequences, highlighting that the rush to innovate must be tempered with a focus on patient safety.

AI in healthcare should not be seen as a panacea but rather as a powerful tool to augment human expertise. No matter how advanced AI becomes, it cannot replace the nuanced judgment and empathy of healthcare providers. The lessons from these case studies underscore the importance of ongoing human oversight, the need for transparency in AI decision-making, and the value of using comprehensive real-world data. The failures of systems like Watson for Oncology and the Epic Sepsis Model, serve as cautionary tales that reveal how critical it is for AI tools to evolve alongside the complex and ever-changing realities of medical practice.

As we look to the future of AI in healthcare, the path forward is clear: innovation must be balanced with rigorous safeguards. Testing AI across diverse settings, ensuring transparency in its decision-making processes, and continuously updating models with the latest medical research are non-negotiable standards that must be upheld. Only by addressing these challenges can we harness the true potential of AI to improve healthcare outcomes, while safeguarding the lives and well-being of patients. In the end, the goal should not to replace human healthcare providers but to empower them with better tools to deliver more effective and personalized care. Through this balanced approach, AI can truly transform healthcare in ways that are safe, equitable, and beneficial for all.

Looking Ahead: The Dark Side of AI — When AI is Used for Malicious Purposes

AI has tremendous potential for good, but as we will see in the next chapter, it can also be used for harmful purposes. From cyberattacks to disinformation campaigns, bad actors are leveraging AI to disrupt industries and societies. We'll examine how AI technologies are being weaponized and discuss strategies for preventing and mitigating the malicious use of AI.

Chapter 11: The Dark Side of AI – When AI is Used for Malicious Purposes

Artificial Intelligence (AI) has the potential to revolutionize industries and improve daily life, but it also harbors significant risks when used maliciously. As AI technology continues to advance, the dark side of AI becomes more pronounced. Criminals, political actors, and rogue developers have harnessed AI's power to engage in cybercrime, disinformation, and fraud. This chapter sheds light on the rising misuse of AI for destructive purposes, exposing how bad actors are exploiting AI for financial gain, political manipulation, and even warfare. The malicious applications of AI reveal vulnerabilities in our digital ecosystems and demonstrate the urgent need for countermeasures, regulations, and ethical standards to ensure the technology is not weaponized.

In recent years, AI has transformed from a tool of innovation to an instrument for sophisticated cybercrime. Voice-cloning fraud, in which AI replicates a person's voice with startling accuracy, has been used to deceive employees and executives into transferring large sums of money. AI-powered phishing attacks now mimic human interaction so effectively that they can manipulate individuals into revealing sensitive information without raising suspicion. Meanwhile, ransomware attacks have become increasingly sophisticated, as AI helps identify weaknesses in networks, allowing attackers to launch more targeted and destructive attacks on critical infrastructure, such as hospitals and financial institutions.

Beyond financial fraud and corporate espionage, AI's role in disinformation campaigns has amplified its potential for societal disruption. Political actors have utilized deepfake technology to create false video or audio content to influence public opinion, destabilize democratic processes, and undermine trust in legitimate sources of information. In parallel, AI-driven bots flood social media platforms with disinformation, spreading false narratives and distorting public discourse on a massive scale. These malicious applications of AI not only threaten the integrity of political systems but also erode public trust in digital content.

We examine a series of cases where AI has been deliberately weaponized to achieve malicious objectives. These include voice-cloning fraud used to carry out high-stakes financial scams, deepfake technologies employed to deceive and manipulate political figures, and AI-driven disinformation bots that influence public opinion and distort online ecosystems. Each of these examples underscores the devastating real-world impact AI can have when it falls into the wrong hands. This chapter highlights the growing urgency for global cooperation, the development of advanced AI detection tools, and the creation of ethical standards to counteract these emerging threats and prevent further exploitation of AI for malicious purposes.

Case Study 1: Fraudsters Use AI to Mimic CEO's Voice in Cybercrime

What Happened:

In March 2019, cybercriminals orchestrated a sophisticated scam using AI-generated voice technology (also known as voice cloning) to defraud a UK-based energy firm. The attackers successfully used AI to mimic the voice of the company's German CEO, instructing a senior executive in the UK to transfer €220,000 to a Hungarian bank account. The AI-cloned voice was convincing enough that the executive never suspected fraud until it was too late. This attack marked a new level of cybercrime sophistication, showing how AI can mimic human speech patterns to deceive even experienced professionals (The Wall Street Journal, 2019).

How AI Was Used:

The fraudsters likely employed deep learning models trained on recordings of the CEO's voice, allowing them to replicate his tone, accent, and speech cadence. By cloning the CEO's voice so convincingly, the criminals exploited a basic human trust mechanism, recognizing and trusting the voices of familiar people. Traditional security protocols, such as verification through phone calls or voice instructions, were rendered ineffective in this case due to the AI's ability to precisely mimic a trusted individual's voice.

Lessons Learned:

This case demonstrates that AI-powered voice cloning can be used for high-stakes financial fraud, emphasizing the need for multi-factor authentication and more robust security measures in business transactions. Companies should adopt layered verification protocols, such as biometric security, and train employees to be aware of AI-enabled threats, especially in high-level financial decision-making.

Case Study 2: Deepfake Caller Poses as Ukrainian Official to U.S. Senator

What Happened:

In 2024, a U.S. senator fell victim to a sophisticated deepfake operation when a caller, posing as a senior Ukrainian official, requested a videoconference under false pretenses. Senator Benjamin L. Cardin, the chairman of the Senate Foreign Relations Committee, was targeted in a Zoom call where an individual appeared to be Dmytro Kuleba, Ukraine's former foreign minister. The deepfake impersonation was so convincing that the senator initially believed he was speaking to the legitimate official.

However, suspicions arose when the deepfake caller began to ask politically charged questions, particularly regarding U.S. foreign policy toward Russia. The impersonator pressed Senator Cardin on his stance on sending long-range missiles into Russian territory, raising red flags. Sensing something was amiss, the senator abruptly ended the call and reported the incident to the State Department. Upon investigation, it was confirmed that the individual posing as Mr. Kuleba was an impersonation, created using advanced deepfake technology (The New York Times, 2024).

How AI Was Used:

The perpetrators relied on deepfake technology, an artificial intelligence-driven method that can manipulate audio and video to create realistic, fabricated representations of real people. In this case, the AI technology successfully created a convincing likeness of the Ukrainian official, including accurate facial features, mannerisms, and voice patterns. The manipulation was so refined that it initially passed as genuine, even under the scrutiny of a seasoned U.S. lawmaker.

Deepfakes typically utilize generative adversarial networks (GANs) to create these forgeries. In GANs, two AI networks, one generating the fake content and the other detecting it compete to create highly convincing fabricated media (Medium, 2019). In this case, the technology was used not to create a viral video for the public but to deceive a high-level political figure in a private setting.

Lessons Learned:

This case underscores the growing threat posed by AI-driven deepfake technology in the realm of political espionage and foreign interference. While deepfakes have previously been used to spread misinformation on social media, such as in a 2022 fake video of Ukrainian President Volodymyr Zelensky surrendering to Russia, this incident represents a more dangerous evolution (Reuters, 2022). Foreign actors, potentially from adversarial states like Russia, have begun using AI to impersonate officials directly in private communications, bypassing the public sphere and attempting to extract sensitive information or influence policy decisions.

The incident highlights the importance of vigilance and caution among public officials. As deepfake technology becomes more advanced and accessible, lawmakers and government personnel must be trained to recognize the signs of AI-generated impersonations. It also underscores the need for enhanced AI detection tools and security protocols, particularly as foreign actors increasingly use these methods to interfere with democratic processes, influence elections, or destabilize international relations.

Case Study 3: AI-Powered Bots in Political Disinformation Campaigns

What Happened:

During the 2016 U.S. Presidential election, AI-powered bots were deployed on social media platforms to spread misinformation, manipulate public opinion, and amplify divisive content. A study published in Nature Communications in 2018 revealed that AI-driven bots played a key role in the spread of disinformation during the election period. These bots, designed to mimic human users, generated and shared false or misleading content at a scale that overwhelmed social media's existing moderation capabilities (Nature Communications, 2018).

How AI Was Used:

The bots likely utilized natural language processing (NLP) algorithms to generate human-like content, including tweets, posts, and comments. The AI-driven bots were programmed to post and share politically charged or misleading content, targeting specific demographics based on data analysis. The bots acted as force multipliers, artificially inflating the popularity of certain messages and narratives by boosting engagement metrics such as likes, shares, and retweets. This led to an echo chamber effect, where misinformation was spread far and wide without being properly vetted.

The research also showed that these bots played a crucial role in amplifying fake news stories, influencing real users to engage with and further disseminate the content. The AI-powered bots manipulated the social media algorithms by creating the appearance of organic engagement, making it harder for platforms to distinguish between real users and bots.

Lessons Learned:

AI-powered bots can significantly impact political discourse and undermine democratic processes by spreading disinformation at a massive scale. Social media platforms must develop better algorithms to detect and neutralize bot activity. Algorithmic transparency, stricter content verification, and policy reform are essential to preventing AI-powered bots from distorting public opinion in future elections.

Advice for Mitigating the Malicious Use of AI:

1. **Strengthening Security Protocols**: Companies should adopt multi-step verification processes for sensitive transactions, especially those involving voice or biometric data, to prevent AI-enabled fraud. Traditional security measures, such as passwords, are no longer sufficient in the face of advanced AI threats like voice cloning. Incorporating multi-factor authentication (MFA) methods such as biometric verification, encrypted token systems, and behavioral analysis can significantly reduce the risk of fraud and enhance overall security.

2. **Developing AI Countermeasures**: Governments, businesses, and tech firms must invest in AI detection tools designed to identify deepfakes and other AI-generated forgeries before they cause harm. Continuous monitoring and the development of advanced detection algorithms are critical to keeping pace with the rapidly evolving sophistication of malicious AI tools. Collaboration between governments and the private sector is necessary to accelerate the development of these countermeasures. Real-time detection and flagging systems, particularly for content spread via social media, can mitigate the rapid dissemination of AI-generated disinformation.

3. **Ethical Guidelines for AI Development**: Developers must adhere to stringent ethical standards to prevent AI from being misused for malicious purposes. Organizations should conduct regular audits and third-party reviews to ensure compliance with ethical AI development practices. This includes promoting transparency in AI systems by creating explainable AI that users can understand and trust. Ethical frameworks should emphasize

fairness, accountability, and the prioritization of human safety over profit or expediency. Additionally, organizations should establish clear boundaries on the acceptable use of AI technologies.

4. Public Education: Raising public awareness of AI-driven fraud, disinformation, and manipulation is crucial for building societal resilience against malicious actors. Educational programs should be designed to teach individuals how to identify AI-generated content, such as deepfakes or automated phishing attempts, and empower them to verify the legitimacy of the information they consume. Media literacy campaigns and school curricula should incorporate lessons on the dangers of AI in the context of disinformation and fraud. By educating the public, we can reduce the effectiveness of these malicious applications and create a more vigilant society.

5. Policy and Regulation: Governments need to collaborate internationally to create and enforce global regulations that hold those who misuse AI technologies accountable. This includes enacting laws that address AI-driven fraud, disinformation, and cybercrime. Regulatory frameworks must evolve alongside technological advancements to ensure that AI tools are not weaponized to exploit vulnerable individuals, institutions, or democratic processes. These regulations should also mandate transparency in the development and deployment of AI systems, especially in sensitive industries such as finance, healthcare, and national security. International cooperation is essential to prevent AI misuse from transcending borders, as bad actors can operate from regions with lax regulations.

Conclusion: Avoiding the Dark Side of AI

As AI technology continues to evolve, its potential for malicious use grows in parallel with its potential for good. From deepfakes to AI-driven fraud, mass phishing attacks, and ransomware, the misuse of AI presents significant challenges to global security, public trust, and democratic integrity. The sophistication of these malicious applications demonstrates that AI is no longer a tool reserved for improving efficiency or driving innovation; it has also become a weapon in the hands of those who wish to disrupt, deceive, and profit at the expense of society.

The examples in this chapter from fraud enabled by AI-cloned voices to deepfake political impersonations and the deployment of AI-powered bots in disinformation campaigns highlight the dangers we face. These case studies are not isolated incidents but part of a growing trend in which AI is used to undermine systems, influence political processes, and exploit vulnerabilities. As these threats evolve, so too must our defenses.

Addressing these risks requires a proactive and multi-pronged approach. Strengthening security protocols such as adopting multi-factor authentication and developing AI detection tools is vital to defending against AI-enabled fraud and espionage. Governments and businesses must invest in countermeasures and regulations that prevent AI from being used maliciously, while ethical guidelines and third-party audits must become standard practice to ensure responsible AI development.

Public education also plays a critical role. Raising awareness about AI-driven threats is essential in creating a digitally literate society that is resilient to manipulation. As AI technologies become increasingly embedded in our lives, the public must be equipped with the knowledge and tools to navigate a world where the lines between reality and deception are increasingly blurred.

Ultimately, the race to innovate must be matched by an equally strong commitment to safeguard society from the risks of AI misuse. The global community, policymakers, industry leaders, and AI developers must work in unison to ensure that AI technologies are used responsibly and ethically, preventing them from becoming tools of exploitation and harm. Only by developing robust countermeasures, creating ethical standards, and enforcing global cooperation can we ensure that AI continues to benefit humanity rather than becoming its undoing.

Looking Ahead: Building Trustworthy and Resilient AI

As we've seen in this chapter, AI technologies hold tremendous potential, but they also present serious risks when misused for malicious purposes. Whether through cyberattacks, disinformation campaigns, or other harmful applications, the darker side of AI underscores the importance of developing systems that can be trusted and that are resilient to failure.

In the next and final chapter, we will explore how organizations can build AI systems that inspire trust by ensuring transparency, safeguarding data, mitigating bias, and adhering to ethical standards. We will also discuss the critical need for resilience in designing AI systems that can adapt to unforeseen challenges, recover from failures, and operate effectively in dynamic environments. The future of AI lies in our ability to balance innovation with the responsibility to create systems that are not only powerful but also safe, equitable, and aligned with societal values.

Conclusion: Building Resilient and Trustworthy AI

As this book has shown, AI failures occur for many reasons spanning various industries, applications, and causes. These failures can impact individuals and groups differently, often disproportionately harming women and those from underrepresented communities, including racial minorities. From biases in decision-making algorithms to flawed data governance and the lack of human oversight, the risks associated with AI failures are significant. These challenges emphasize the urgent need for AI systems that are both resilient and trustworthy.

Resilience in AI refers to the ability of systems to adapt to unforeseen circumstances, learn from mistakes, and recover quickly from failures. This ensures that AI systems can operate effectively in dynamic environments, handling the complexities and uncertainties of real-world conditions. At the same time, trustworthiness is equally crucial. **Trustworthy** AI strives to ensure that systems are transparent, ethical, and equitable in their operation, ensuring that users can rely on them to make fair and responsible decisions.

Throughout this book, we have explored the consequences of AI failures in various sectors, including healthcare, finance, law enforcement, and hiring. These failures have not only undermined the reliability of AI systems but also highlighted the ethical, legal, and societal risks posed by flawed AI deployment. However, by addressing the root causes of these failures, we can build AI systems that are both resilient and trustworthy systems that can adapt, recover, and improve over time while maintaining ethical and transparent practices.

Trust and resilience in AI are built on eight foundational pillars that are critical to ensuring both the technical reliability and the ethical soundness of AI systems:

1. Transparency: AI systems must be open and explainable, allowing users to understand how decisions are made. Transparency is essential not only for building trust but also for enabling quick diagnosis and recovery when systems fail.

2. Fairness and Equity: AI must be designed to avoid bias and ensure that it treats all individuals and groups fairly. This requires rigorous testing and ongoing audits to ensure that the system performs equitably across diverse populations and scenarios.

3. Accountability: Clear frameworks must be in place to hold AI systems and their creators accountable for their outcomes. This ensures that when failures occur, they are swiftly addressed, and improvements are made to prevent future issues.

4. Security and Privacy: AI systems must rigorously protect sensitive data and comply with privacy regulations to maintain public trust. Secure systems are resilient to data breaches and cyberattacks, ensuring the integrity of the data they rely on.

5. Accuracy and Reliability: AI systems must deliver accurate, consistent, and dependable results, particularly in high-stakes contexts. Reliable systems are resilient, capable of adapting to new data and conditions without sacrificing performance.

6. Legal Compliance: AI must adhere to laws and regulations to ensure that it is used responsibly and within legal boundaries. A resilient AI system is flexible enough to adapt to evolving legal standards while continuing to function effectively.

7. Ethical Design: AI must be guided by ethical principles that prioritize human welfare, dignity, and fairness. Ethical AI systems should be resilient in that they are built to prevent harm and can adapt to societal changes in ways that continue to promote fairness and justice.

8. Human Oversight: Human oversight is crucial to ensure that AI systems function appropriately and ethically, particularly in high-stakes decisions that affect people's lives. AI systems must support human judgment, not replace it, ensuring that human experts can intervene when needed, especially when the system encounters ambiguous or unforeseen circumstances. Human oversight enhances resilience by ensuring that AI decisions are scrutinized and validated, reducing the risk of unintended harm.

In this final chapter, we delve deeper into these pillars, discussing how organizations can embed them into their AI strategies to create systems that inspire confidence, operate ethically, and deliver reliable, equitable outcomes. By addressing these foundational principles, organizations can build AI systems that not only perform effectively but also earn the trust of users, regulators, and the broader public.

Trust and resilience in AI are built on eight foundational pillars:

1. Transparency: The Key to Trust and Recovery

Transparency is the cornerstone of trustworthy AI. Without transparency, users and stakeholders are left in the dark about how decisions are made, making it difficult to trust the system. When AI operates in a "black box" fashion, where the underlying logic and decision-making processes are hidden or too complex to explain, people may not be able to adequately assess its fairness, reliability, or accuracy. In sectors like healthcare, finance, or criminal justice, where the consequences of AI decisions can be life-changing, transparency is indispensable.

Transparency also enhances resilience by allowing the system to be evaluated and corrected when errors occur. A transparent system can provide insights into where it went wrong, allowing for faster recovery and better long-term performance.

Why Transparency is Critical:

- **Explainability**: AI systems must be able to articulate why they made a particular decision, whether diagnosing a disease, approving a loan, or identifying a suspect. Explainability helps users understand the reasoning behind the decision and trust its outcome.
- **Accountability through Understanding**: Transparent AI allows regulators, developers, and end-users to audit the system, identify potential biases or errors, and improve performance. This is essential for building a feedback loop that continually enhances the system's reliability.

How to Achieve Transparency:

- **Develop Explainable AI Models**: Not all AI models are inherently transparent, especially complex systems like deep neural networks. However, by using techniques such as post-hoc explanations, feature importance visualization, and interpretable algorithms, developers can offer insights into how AI makes its decisions. This helps bridge the gap between complex AI systems and the need for understandable decision-making.
- **Provide Clear Documentation and User Education**: AI systems should come with clear documentation that explains their capabilities, limitations, and decision-making processes. Users need to be trained or provided with resources that allow them to understand the system's functioning and limitations.

Transparent AI fosters trust by demystifying complex algorithms and providing clarity on how AI arrives at decisions, making the technology more accessible and accountable. When AI systems are open and explainable, they are also easier to monitor, repair, and improve thus increasing their resilience.

2. Fairness and Equity: Ensuring Ethical and Resilient Outcomes

As AI becomes increasingly integrated into decision-making processes that affect real lives, ensuring that these systems produce fair and equitable outcomes is paramount. AI systems risk perpetuating or even exacerbating societal biases if they are trained on flawed or biased data. This is especially dangerous in fields like hiring, lending, policing, and healthcare, where biased decisions can have profound and lasting consequences on individuals or communities.

Resilient AI systems must also be fair. If they are designed to be adaptable and flexible, they can mitigate the risks of bias by continuously learning and adjusting to new data. Building fairness into AI systems ensures that they can produce equitable outcomes across a wide range of scenarios, making them not only trustworthy but also capable of recovering from bias-related failures.

The Risk of Bias:

- **Data Bias**: AI systems are only as good as the data they are trained on. If historical data reflects societal inequities such as gender discrimination in hiring or racial disparities in criminal sentencing, AI systems can inadvertently reinforce those patterns. For example, an AI system used for hiring might learn to favor male candidates if it is trained on data where men were historically preferred.
- **Harmful Outcomes**: Biased AI systems can lead to unfair outcomes, such as denying a mortgage based on race or

assigning a harsher sentence to a defendant because of their ethnicity. Such biases not only harm individuals but also erode public trust in AI as a fair and objective tool.

How to Ensure Fairness and Resilience:

- **Diversify Training Data**: AI systems must be trained on datasets that represent the diversity of the populations they serve. This means including data from different genders, races, socioeconomic backgrounds, and geographic regions to ensure that the AI makes decisions that are fair across demographic lines.
- **Implement Bias Detection and Mitigation**: Regular audits are essential to detect and correct biases in AI systems. Bias mitigation techniques, such as reweighting certain data points or using fairness constraints during model training, can help ensure that AI systems generate equitable outcomes.
- **Hold Developers Accountable for Fairness**: Developers must be conscious of the societal impact of their AI systems. This means building fairness into the design process from the start, rather than treating it as an afterthought.

AI has the potential to reduce human biases, but only if fairness and equity are made a priority in its design and deployment. By focusing on fairness, organizations can ensure that AI systems contribute to social justice rather than perpetuating inequality. AI systems that can recover from bias and learn from mistakes are better positioned to maintain public trust and relevance over time.

3. Accountability: Ensuring Responsibility in AI Systems

Accountability is essential for ensuring that when AI systems fail or cause harm, those responsible can be identified and held to account. As AI systems become more autonomous and integrated into decision-making processes, the question of who is responsible for AI-generated decisions becomes critical. Without clear accountability frameworks, there is a risk that organizations or individuals could shirk responsibility for harmful outcomes caused by AI.

Accountability also contributes to resilience. When clear lines of responsibility are established, it becomes easier to identify and address failures quickly. This ensures that AI systems can recover more effectively from errors and be continually improved based on feedback.

Why Accountability is Important:

- **Avoiding the Accountability Gap**: When AI systems make mistakes, who is responsible, the developer, the organization that deployed the system, or the end-user? A lack of clear accountability structures can lead to "blame-shifting" or the so-called "accountability gap," where no one takes responsibility for AI-caused harm. This is particularly concerning in high-stakes areas like healthcare, where an AI misdiagnosis could lead to serious consequences.
- **Legal and Ethical Ramifications**: As governments begin to regulate AI more heavily, accountability will become even more important. Organizations will need to ensure that their AI systems comply with legal standards and that they have procedures in place for addressing any harm caused by AI.

How to Establish Accountability:

- **Assign Responsibility at Every Stage**: AI accountability should be built into the system from the beginning, with clear roles and responsibilities assigned to developers, users, and organizations. This ensures that if something goes wrong, it's easy to trace responsibility and take corrective action.

- **Audit and Document AI Decisions**: AI systems should keep detailed logs of their decisions and the reasoning behind them. This helps create an audit trail that allows organizations to review AI outcomes and identify where mistakes occurred.
- **Establish AI Governance Structures**: Organizations should create AI governance frameworks that include oversight committees, ethical review boards, and regular audits to ensure AI systems are meeting legal, ethical, and performance standards.

Accountability ensures that organizations take responsibility for their AI systems and actively work to prevent harm, thereby building trust with users and stakeholders. Clear accountability mechanisms also make AI systems more resilient, as they allow for swift identification and correction of problems.

4. Security and Privacy: Safeguarding Data in the Age of AI

As AI systems become more data-hungry, they are processing increasing amounts of sensitive personal information, from medical records to financial data to social media activity. With this rise in data usage comes the heightened risk of data breaches, cyberattacks, and privacy violations. For AI to be trustworthy and resilient, it must rigorously protect this data and comply with the strictest privacy regulations.

Security and privacy are fundamental to resilience because a system that is vulnerable to breaches is inherently unstable. A single data breach or privacy violation can erode user trust and disrupt the system's functionality, causing long-term damage to its reputation and operation.

Why Security and Privacy Matter:

- **Data Breaches**: AI systems are prime targets for hackers due to the sheer volume of sensitive information they process. A data breach can expose personal, financial, or medical information, leading to identity theft, fraud, or serious reputational damage to organizations.
- **Erosion of Trust**: If users fear that their data is not secure or that it will be misused, they will be less willing to engage with AI systems. AI can only operate effectively in environments where users feel confident that their personal information is safe and private.

How to Protect Security and Privacy:

- **Encrypt and Anonymize Data**: AI systems must encrypt data both in transit and at rest to protect it from unauthorized access. Anonymization techniques can also be used to ensure that personal data is not easily traceable back to individuals, thus safeguarding privacy.
- **Implement Data Minimization Practices**: Organizations should collect only the data they need for AI to function and avoid hoarding unnecessary information. This reduces the risk of data breaches and minimizes the potential for privacy violations.
- **Adhere to Privacy Regulations**: Compliance with data protection laws, such as the General Data Protection Regulation (GDPR), is crucial for building trust. These regulations require organizations to handle data transparently, give users control over their personal data, and report breaches when they occur.

By protecting data and prioritizing privacy, organizations can build AI systems that users trust to handle their most sensitive information responsibly. A secure AI system is a resilient onc able to maintain its operations and protect users' information even in the face of external threats.

5. Accuracy and Reliability: Ensuring AI Performs as Expected

No matter how ethical, transparent, or fair an AI system is, it will not be trusted if it doesn't perform accurately and reliably. In high-stakes environments like healthcare, law enforcement, or financial services, the consequences of AI errors can be catastrophic. Therefore, accuracy and reliability are fundamental to building trust in AI.

Resilient AI systems must be capable of adapting to changes in their environment while maintaining a high level of accuracy. This involves continuous testing, monitoring, and improvement to ensure that the system remains reliable and effective even when new challenges arise.

Why Accuracy and Reliability Matter:

- **Trust in Performance**: Users must be able to rely on AI systems to consistently perform their tasks accurately. For example, an AI system used in healthcare must provide accurate diagnoses; otherwise, it could lead to misdiagnosis and harm to patients. Similarly, an AI system used in financial trading must make reliable predictions, or it could result in significant financial losses.
- **Preventing Errors**: Inaccurate or unreliable AI systems not only erode trust but also pose significant risks, especially when deployed at scale. Regular monitoring and rigorous testing are needed to ensure that AI systems perform as expected under various conditions.

How to Ensure Accuracy and Reliability:

- **Thorough Testing and Validation**: AI systems must undergo extensive testing before they are deployed in real-world environments. This includes testing the system's performance across a wide range of scenarios to ensure that it can handle different inputs and conditions.
- **Continuous Monitoring and Updates**: Once deployed, AI systems must be continuously monitored to ensure they maintain their accuracy over time. This includes regular updates to ensure the system stays current with new data, market conditions, or medical research.
- **High-Quality Data Inputs**: The accuracy of AI systems is highly dependent on the quality of the data they receive. Organizations must ensure that the data fed into AI systems is accurate, clean, and up to date to ensure reliable outcomes.

Accuracy and reliability are essential to building trust in AI, ensuring that users can depend on the technology to make correct decisions in critical areas. Reliable systems are more resilient, as they can handle diverse and evolving scenarios while maintaining their performance.

6. Legal Compliance: Aligning AI with Regulatory Frameworks

AI technologies are evolving at a rapid pace, often outstripping the development of laws and regulations meant to govern their use. However, as AI becomes more integrated into industries and public services, adhering to legal standards is crucial to prevent misuse, discrimination, or other harmful outcomes. AI must operate within clear legal frameworks that protect individual rights, ensure safety, and prevent unethical practices.

Resilient AI systems must be capable of adapting to changing legal standards. As regulations evolve, these systems should be flexible enough to comply with new rules while continuing to function effectively.

Why Legal Compliance is Crucial:

- **Avoiding Legal Repercussions**: Organizations that fail to ensure their AI systems comply with the law face the risk of lawsuits, fines, and regulatory sanctions. In Europe, for instance, the GDPR imposes heavy fines for breaches of data privacy. In the U.S., laws governing AI usage in healthcare or finance impose strict regulatory requirements that must be followed.
- **Ensuring Ethical Use**: Legal compliance ensures that AI systems are used responsibly and ethically, protecting individuals from discriminatory or harmful practices. Laws governing data protection, equal opportunity, and anti-discrimination ensure that AI systems do not cause harm or infringe upon individual rights.

How to Ensure Legal Compliance:

- **Stay Updated with Regulations**: As AI regulations continue to evolve globally, organizations must stay informed about the latest legal requirements in their industry or region. Regular compliance reviews should be conducted to ensure that AI systems align with applicable laws.
- **Collaborate with Legal Experts**: AI development teams should work closely with legal experts to navigate the regulatory landscape and ensure compliance. This collaboration ensures that AI systems are designed with legal safeguards in mind from the outset.
- **Document and Audit AI Decisions**: Keeping detailed records of how AI systems make decisions can help organizations defend themselves in the event of regulatory scrutiny or legal

action. These records also help improve transparency and accountability.

Legal compliance not only ensures that AI systems operate within established guidelines but also helps strengthen their resilience to changes in the legal landscape. By proactively building systems with compliance in mind, organizations can create a flexible framework that allows for smoother adaptation to new regulations. This flexibility enables AI systems to update their processes and features in response to legal changes without requiring extensive modifications or disrupting functionality.

7. Ethical Design: Prioritizing Human Welfare and Resilience

Beyond legal compliance, AI systems must also adhere to broader ethical standards. Ethical AI is about more than just avoiding harm, it is about actively promoting the welfare of individuals and society. Ethical AI systems are designed to respect human dignity, protect vulnerable groups, and ensure fairness. In a world where AI can influence everything from job opportunities to medical treatment, ethical design is crucial for creating systems that are not only effective but also just.

Ethical AI is also resilient. By prioritizing fairness, transparency, and human welfare, organizations can build systems that can adapt to societal changes and challenges, continuing to deliver positive outcomes even in the face of ethical dilemmas.

Why Ethical Design Matters:

- **AI Impacts Human Lives**: AI systems influence decisions that can affect people's rights, opportunities, and well-being. Ensuring that AI is designed with ethical considerations from the outset can prevent harm and promote positive outcomes.
- **Building Public Trust**: Organizations that prioritize ethics in AI design will gain the trust of their users and the public. Ethical

AI fosters positive relationships between technology providers and the communities they serve, ensuring that AI adoption is driven by mutual benefit.

How to Ensure Ethical AI Design:

- **Embed Ethics in the Development Process**: Ethical considerations should not be an afterthought, they should be integrated into every stage of AI development. This includes assessing the potential societal impacts of AI, anticipating how it might be misused, and designing safeguards to prevent harm.
- **Create Ethical Guidelines and Governance**: Organizations should establish ethical guidelines for AI development and deploy governance structures to oversee the ethical use of AI. These guidelines should reflect the organization's commitment to fairness, transparency, and respect for individual rights.
- **Involve Diverse Stakeholders**: Ethical AI development requires input from a broad range of stakeholders, including ethicists, legal experts, industry professionals, and representatives from affected communities. This ensures that diverse perspectives are considered, and the AI system is aligned with societal values.

Ethical design ensures that AI systems operate in ways that are fair, transparent, and beneficial to all users. By prioritizing ethics, organizations can build AI systems that are not only trusted but also resilient, capable of handling ethical dilemmas and evolving in ways that continue to benefit society.

8. Human Oversight: Balancing AI Autonomy with Human Judgment

While AI systems can automate many complex processes, human oversight is essential to ensure that these systems operate ethically, responsibly, and reliably. AI should support and augment human decision-making rather than replace it, particularly in high-stakes industries like healthcare, transportation, and law enforcement. In situations where AI decisions impact fundamental human rights, safety, or freedoms, human intervention is critical to prevent harm and ensure fairness.

Resilient AI systems must be designed to incorporate human oversight at key decision points. By integrating human judgment into the AI workflow, organizations can ensure that systems are capable of handling unforeseen circumstances and ethical dilemmas, while reducing the risk of errors and unintended consequences.

Why Human Oversight is Crucial:

- **Validation and Interpretation**: Human experts can validate AI outputs, ensuring that decisions are accurate and appropriate, especially in complex or high-stakes scenarios.
- **Ethical Safeguards**: Human oversight provides a crucial check against biased or unethical decisions, ensuring that AI systems uphold principles of fairness and justice.
- **Intervention in Failures**: AI systems may encounter unforeseen situations that they cannot handle effectively. Human intervention is necessary to address system failures and mitigate their impact.

How to Implement Human Oversight:

- **Design AI to Support Human Decision-Making**: AI systems should augment human capabilities, offering insights and recommendations while allowing human experts to make the final decision.
- **Establish Clear Escalation Protocols**: Define specific scenarios where human intervention is mandatory, particularly in areas where decisions affect human rights or involve life-and-death consequences.
- **Continuous Monitoring and Review**: Human oversight should be ongoing. Monitoring AI systems in real time ensures that humans can intervene quickly when issues arise, maintaining the system's reliability and ethical integrity.

Incorporating human oversight enhances the resilience of AI systems by ensuring they are not solely reliant on algorithmic decision-making. It allows for more flexible, adaptive systems capable of learning from human input and responding effectively to complex, real-world challenges.

Conclusion: Building Resilient and Trustworthy AI

As we conclude this book, it is clear that the journey to building resilient and trustworthy AI is not a straightforward one. Throughout this book, we have examined various AI failures, from biased algorithms and data governance issues to the lack of human oversight and ethical blind spots. These failures have underscored the complexities and challenges inherent in designing AI systems that are capable of navigating the diverse and often unpredictable real-world environments in which they operate.

Yet, while the risks of AI failures are substantial, the potential benefits of AI are immense. AI holds the promise of revolutionizing industries, improving efficiency, and solving some of the most pressing global challenges, from healthcare to environmental sustainability. The key to realizing this potential lies in our ability to build AI systems that are both resilient to failure and trustworthy in their operation.

Building AI that is resilient means more than just ensuring it functions correctly in ideal circumstances. It involves preparing AI to handle uncertainty, unexpected scenarios, and changing environments. It requires systems that can adapt, learn from mistakes, and evolve in real-time. Resilient AI is capable of absorbing shocks, such as biased inputs or flawed data, and adjusting its outputs accordingly without causing widespread disruption or harm. It means creating AI that is robust enough to withstand the complexities of the real world, where perfect data rarely exists, and unanticipated edge cases are the norm.

At the same time, AI must be trustworthy. A system that works technically but cannot be relied upon to make ethical or unbiased decisions is a system that will not earn the confidence of its users or the wider society. Trustworthy AI prioritizes fairness, transparency, and accountability. It recognizes that algorithms do not operate in a vacuum but rather affect people's lives in profound ways. Whether it's a diagnostic tool in a hospital, a predictive model in the criminal justice system, or an algorithm that determines financial lending, AI must be built on the foundation of trust if it is to be used responsibly and adopted widely.

The challenge, then, is balancing these dual imperatives of resilience and trustworthiness. A system that is only resilient but not trustworthy may still cause harm, perpetuating biases and making opaque decisions that erode public trust. Conversely, a system that is trustworthy but not resilient may collapse under pressure or fail to adapt to new challenges. The future of AI depends on our ability to develop systems that are both, systems that can not only withstand the rigors of real-world application but also operate in ways that are fair, transparent, and accountable.

Achieving this balance requires an ongoing commitment from AI developers, policymakers, and organizations alike. It demands that we continuously monitor and audit AI systems, ensuring that they are performing ethically and effectively, even as they evolve. It requires dedication to refining data practices, mitigating bias, and embedding human oversight in AI deployment. And perhaps most importantly, it calls for the recognition that AI is not a static technology but a dynamic, ever-evolving force that must be carefully nurtured and shaped to serve humanity's best interests.

The road ahead is complex, but it is also filled with possibility. If we can meet the challenges of resilience and trustworthiness head-on, the rewards will be transformative, not only for the industries and sectors that adopt AI but for society as a whole. By striving to build AI systems that are both resilient in the face of failure and deeply rooted in ethical principles, we can unlock the full potential of this technology and ensure that it benefits everyone equitably.

Wrapping Up: The Future of AI

The future of AI is bright, but it is also fraught with challenges. As we continue to develop and deploy AI systems, it is essential to remember that these technologies do not exist in isolation. They impact real people, influence important decisions, and shape the world in profound ways. As such, building resilient and trustworthy AI is not just a technical challenge, it is a moral imperative.

By focusing on resilience, we ensure that AI systems can withstand the challenges and uncertainties of the real world, adapting to new data, recovering from failures, and improving over time. By prioritizing trustworthiness, we build systems that are transparent, fair, ethical, and accountable systems that users can rely on, and society can embrace.

This book has explored the many reasons why AI systems fail and the often-devastating consequences of those failures. But it has also offered insights for mitigating those risks. Through careful design, robust testing, and a commitment to the foundational pillars of transparency, fairness, accountability, security, accuracy, legal compliance, and ethics, we can build AI systems that truly serve humanity, enhancing our lives, solving critical challenges, and advancing the common good.

As we look toward the future, the responsibility rests with all of us AI developers, policymakers, industry leaders, and society at large to ensure that AI fulfills its promise. By building resilient and trustworthy AI systems, we can unlock the full potential of this transformative technology while safeguarding against its risks. In doing so, we pave the way for a future where AI serves as a powerful, reliable, and ethical force for good.

Glossary of Key AI Terms

Algorithm: A step-by-step procedure or set of rules designed to solve problems, often used in computing to process data and make decisions.

Bias: A systematic error introduced into a system or decision-making process, often resulting from incomplete or skewed data.

Anonymization: The process of removing personal identifiers from datasets to protect privacy.

Audit Trail: A record of how decisions are made, useful for accountability and transparency in any system.

Autonomous Systems: Systems capable of operating independently without human intervention, such as self-driving cars or drones.

Black Box: A system or process whose internal workings are not visible or understandable, raising concerns about accountability and transparency.

Bias Mitigation: Techniques used to reduce or eliminate bias in systems to ensure fair outcomes.

Data Quality: The accuracy, completeness, and reliability of data used in decision-making processes.

Ethical AI: The practice of designing AI systems that prioritize fairness, accountability, and transparency, minimizing harm and bias.

Machine Learning: A subset of artificial intelligence where systems learn and improve from experience without being explicitly programmed.

Overfitting: A modeling error that occurs when a system is too closely aligned with its training data, leading to poor generalization to new data.

Underfitting: A scenario where a model is too simplistic and fails to capture underlying patterns, leading to poor performance.

Model Transparency: The extent to which the workings and decision-making processes of a model are understandable and explainable.

Supervised Learning: A type of machine learning where the system is trained on labeled data to predict outcomes or classify new data.

Unsupervised Learning: A type of machine learning where the system identifies patterns or groupings in data without being given labeled outcomes.

References

1. ACLU (2018). "Amazon's face recognition falsely matched 28 members of Congress with mugshots." Available at: https://www.aclu.org/news/privacy-technology/amazons-face-recognition-falsely-matched-28
2. AFR (2024). "Black George Washington? Google Shows Pitfalls of Woke AI." Available at: https://www.afr.com/technology/black-george-washington-google-shows-pitfalls-of-woke-ai-20240229-p5f8ob
3. AI Incident Database. (2024). AI Incident Database Editor's Guide. Retrieved from https://incidentdatabase.ai/editors-guide/
4. BBC (2024). "Why Google's 'woke' AI problem won't be an easy fix". Available at: https://www.bbc.com/news/technology-68412620
5. BBC News (2015). "Google apologises for Photos app's racist blunder." Available at: https://www.bbc.com/news/technology-33347866
6. BBC News (2018). "Amazon tool flags Congress members as suspects." Available at: https://www.bbc.com/news/technology-44965154
7. BBC News (2022). "Meta settles Cambridge Analytica scandal case for $725m." Available at: https://www.bbc.com/news/technology-64075067
8. BBC News (2024). "Airline held liable for its chatbot giving passenger bad advice - what this means for travellers." Available at: https://www.bbc.com/travel/article/20240222-air-canada-chatbot-misinformation-what-travellers-should-know
9. Buolamwini, J., & Gebru, T. (2018). "Gender shades: Intersectional accuracy disparities in commercial gender classification." Proceedings of Machine Learning Research, 81, 1–15. Available at: https://proceedings.mlr.press/v81/buolamwini18a/buolamwini18a.pdf
10. CBS News (2018). "#DeleteFacebook trends amid Cambridge Analytica scandal." Available at: https://www.cbsnews.com/news/deletefacebook-trends-amid-cambridge-analytica-scandal/
11. Centers for Medicare & Medicaid Services (CMS). (2024). "FAQs Related to Coverage Criteria and Utilization Management Requirements in CMS Final Rule (CMS-4201-F)." Available at: https://cdn.arstechnica.net/wp-content/uploads/2024/02/cms-memo-2624-faqs-related-to-coverage-criteria-and-utilization-management-requirements-in-cms-final-rule-cms-4201-f.pdf

12. CNBC (2017). "JPMorgan Suffers Losses Due to AI Trading Missteps." Available at: https://www.cnbc.com/2017/05/11/jpmorgan-ai-trading.html
13. CNBC (2018). "Facebook-Cambridge Analytica: A timeline of the data hijacking scandal." Available at: https://www.cnbc.com/2018/04/10/facebook-cambridge-analytica-a-timeline-of-the-data-hijacking-scandal.html
14. CNBC (2024). "Tesla settles lawsuit over Autopilot crash that killed Apple engineer." Available at: https://www.cnbc.com/2024/04/08/tesla-settles-wrongful-death-lawsuit-over-fatal-2018-autopilot-crash.html
15. CNN (2021). "Zillow is exiting the home-flipping business, laying off 25% of its staff." Available at: https://edition.cnn.com/2021/11/02/homes/zillow-exit-ibuying-home-business/index.html
16. CNN (2023). "Uber self-driving car test driver pleads guilty to endangerment in pedestrian death case." Available at: https://edition.cnn.com/2023/07/29/business/uber-self-driving-car-death-guilty/index.html
17. Dressel, J. and Farid, H. (2018). The accuracy, fairness, and limits of predicting recidivism. Science Advances, 4(1), eaao5580. Available at: https://www.ncbi.nlm.nih.gov/pmc/articles/PMC5777393/pdf/aao5580.pdf
18. Duke Today (2017). “Opening the Lid on Criminal Sentencing Software”. Available at: https://today.duke.edu/2017/07/opening-lid-criminal-sentencing-software
19. Federal Aviation Administration. (2020). “Summary of the FAA’s Review of the Boeing 737 MAX”. Retrieved from https://www.faa.gov/sites/faa.gov/files/2022-08/737_RTS_Summary.pdf
20. Future Farming (2023). "John Deere enables targeted spraying on weeds." Available at: https://www.futurefarming.com/crop-solutions/weed-pest-control/john-deere-enables-targeted-spraying-on-weeds/
21. Future of Life Institute (2021). "The Financial World and AI." Available at: https://futureoflife.org/recent-news/financial-world-ai/
22. Ginsberg J, Mohebbi M, Patel R, et al. (2009). "Detecting Influenza Epidemics Using Search Engine Query Data." Nature 457, 1012–1014. Available at: https://doi.org/10.1038/nature07634
23. Harvard Business Review (2023). "What Smart Companies Know About

Integrating AI." Available at: https://hbr.org/2023/07/what-smart-companies-know-about-integrating-ai
24. Human Rights Watch. (2020). "Stopping Killer Robots: Country Positions on Banning Fully Autonomous Weapons and Retaining Human Control". Available at: https://www.hrw.org/sites/default/files/media_2021/04/arms0820_web_1.pdf
25. Lazer, D., et al. (2014). "The Parable of Google Flu: Traps in Big Data Analysis." Science. Available at: https://gking.harvard.edu/files/gking/files/0314policyforumff.pdf
26. Lighthouse Labs (2020). "How Netflix Utilises Data Science." Available at: https://www.lighthouselabs.ca/en/blog/how-netflix-uses-data-to-optimize-their-product#:~:text=Netflix%20began%20experimenting%20with%20data,beyond%20rating%20prediction%20and%20into
27. Lyons PG, Hofford MR, Yu SC, et al. "Factors Associated With Variability in the Performance of a Proprietary Sepsis Prediction Model Across 9 Networked Hospitals in the US". JAMA Intern Med. 2023;183(6):611–612. Available at: https://jamanetwork.com/journals/jamainternalmedicine/article-abstract/2803492?resultClick=1
28. McGregor, S. (2021). Preventing repeated real-world AI failures by cataloging incidents: The AI Incident Database. In Proceedings of the Thirty-Third Annual Conference on Innovative Applications of Artificial Intelligence (IAAI-21). Virtual Conference. Available at: https://incidentdatabase.ai/
29. Medium (2019). "The Rise of Deepfake Videos: Unraveling the Magic Behind GANs," by O. Hermans. Available at: https://medium.com/@ohermans1/the-rise-of-deepfake-videos-unraveling-the-magic-behind-gans-a4d7c03637fa
30. Microsoft. (2016). "Learning from Tay's introduction". [online] Available at: https://blogs.microsoft.com/blog/2016/03/25/learning-tays-introduction/
31. National Transportation Safety Board (2019). "Collision Between Vehicle Controlled by Developmental Automated Driving System and Pedestrian". Available at:

https://www.ntsb.gov/investigations/AccidentReports/Reports/HAR1903.pdf
32. National Transportation Safety Board (2020). "Collision Between a Sport Utnility Vehicle Operating With Partial Driving Automation and a Crash Attenuator, Mountain View, California, March 23, 2018". Available at: https://www.ntsb.gov/investigations/AccidentReports/Reports/HAR2001.pdf
33. Nature Communications (2018). "The Role of Bots in Amplifying Misinformation During the 2016 US Election." Available at: https://www.nature.com/articles/s41467-018-06930-7
34. News.com.au (2020). "How a 'confused' AI may have fought pilots attempting to save Boeing 737 MAX8s." Available at: https://www.news.com.au/technology/innovation/inventions/how-a-confused-ai-may-have-fought-pilots-attempting-to-save-boeing-737-max8s/news-story/bf0d102f699905e5aa8d1f6d65f4c27e
35. New York Department of Financial Services (2021). "DFS Issues Findings on the Apple Card and Its Underwriter Goldman Sachs Bank." Available at: https://www.dfs.ny.gov/reports_and_publications/press_releases/pr202103231
36. Office of the Australian Information Commissioner (2021). "Statement on Clearview AI." Available at: https://www.oaic.gov.au/news/media-centre/statement-on-clearview-ai
37. Politico (2020). "How Cambridge Analytica Used AI." Available at: https://www.politico.eu/newsletter/ai-decoded/politico-ai-decoded-how-cambridge-analytica-used-ai-no-google-didnt-call-for-a-ban-on-face-recognition-restricting-ai-exports/
38. ProPublica (2016). "How We Analyzed the COMPAS Recidivism Algorithm." Available at: https://www.propublica.org/article/how-we-analyzed-the-compas-recidivism-algorithm
39. Reese, H. (2016). "Why Microsoft's Tay AI bot went wrong". Available at: https://www.techrepublic.com/article/why-microsofts-tay-ai-bot-went-wrong/
40. Reuters (2018). "Amazon Scraps Secret AI Recruiting Tool That Showed Bias Against Women." Available at: https://www.reuters.com/article/world/amazon-scraps-secret-ai-recruiting-tool-that-showed-bias-against-women-idUSKCN1MK08J

41. Reuters (2019). "Facebook to pay record $5 billion U.S. fine over privacy, faces antitrust probe." Available at: https://www.reuters.com/article/technology/facebook-to-pay-record-5-billion-us-fine-over-privacy-faces-antitrust-probe-idUSKCN1UJ1L9

42. Reuters (2022). "Deepfake Footage Purports to Show Ukrainian President Capitulating." Available at: https://www.reuters.com/world/europe/deepfake-footage-purports-show-ukrainian-president-capitulating-2022-03-16/

43. Roberts, M., Driggs, D., Thorpe, M. et al. "Common pitfalls and recommendations for using machine learning to detect and prognosticate for COVID-19 using chest radiographs and CT scans." Nat Mach Intell 3, 199–217 (2021). Available at: https://doi.org/10.1038/s42256-021-00307-0

44. RSNA (2020). "Artificial Intelligence and Human Life: Five lessons for Radiology from the 737 MAX Disasters." Available at: https://pubs.rsna.org/doi/pdf/10.1148/ryai.2020190111

45. Schertz AR, Lenoir KM, Bertoni AG, Levine BJ, Mongraw-Chaffin M, Thomas KW. (2023). "Sepsis Prediction Model for Determining Sepsis vs SIRS, qSOFA, and SOFA." JAMA Network Open. Available at: https://jamanetwork.com/journals/jamanetworkopen/fullarticle/2808756

46. Slaw (2020). "Artificial Intelligence, Algorithmic Racism, and the Canadian Criminal Justice System". Available at: https://www.slaw.ca/2020/10/26/artificial-intelligence-algorithmic-racism-and-the-canadian-criminal-justice-system/

47. Stanford Graduate School of Business (2021). "Flip or Flop? Why Zillow's Algorithmic Home-Buying Venture Imploded." Available at: https://www.gsb.stanford.edu/insights/flip-flop-why-zillows-algorithmic-home-buying-venture-imploded

48. Stat News (2018). "IBM Watson Recommended 'Unsafe and Incorrect' Cancer Treatments." Available at: https://www.statnews.com/2018/07/25/ibm-watson-recommended-unsafe-incorrect-treatments/

49. TechHQ (2024). "Air Canada Refund for Customer Who Used Chatbot." Available at: https://techhq.com/2024/02/air-canada-refund-for-customer-who-used-chatbot/

50. The Estate of Gene B. Lokken and The Estate of Dale Henry Tetzloff, individually and on behalf of all others similarly situated v. UnitedHealth Group, Inc., UnitedHealthcare, Inc., naviHealth, Inc., and Does 1-50, inclusive, Civil File No. 23-cv-03514-JRT-DTS (D. Minn. filed Nov. 14, 2023). Available at: https://fingfx.thomsonreuters.com/gfx/legaldocs/lbvgoerodvq/Lokken%20v%20UnitedHealth%20complaint%2011-14.pdf

51. The Guardian (2015). "Women less likely to be shown ads for high-paid jobs on Google, study shows." Available at: https://www.theguardian.com/technology/2015/jul/08/women-less-likely-ads-high-paid-jobs-google-study

52. The Guardian (2016). "Microsoft 'deeply sorry' for offensive tweets by AI chatbot." Available at: https://www.theguardian.com/technology/2016/mar/26/microsoft-deeply-sorry-for-offensive-tweets-by-ai-chatbot

53. The Guardian (2018a). "Uber halts self-driving tests after pedestrian killed in Arizona." Available at: https://www.theverge.com/2018/3/19/17139518/uber-self-driving-car-fatal-crash-tempe-arizona

54. The Guardian (2018b). "Amazon ditched AI recruiting tool that favored men for technical jobs." Available at: https://www.theguardian.com/technology/2018/oct/10/amazon-hiring-ai-gender-bias-recruiting-engine

55. The Guardian (2018c). "Cambridge Analytica closing down after Facebook row, reports say." Available at: https://amp.theguardian.com/uk-news/2018/may/02/cambridge-analytica-closing-down-after-facebook-row-reports-say

56. The Guardian (2018d). "Revealed: 50 million Facebook profiles harvested for Cambridge Analytica in major data breach." Available at: https://www.theguardian.com/news/2018/mar/17/cambridge-analytica-facebook-influence-us-election

57. The Guardian (2024). "Tesla's Autopilot Fatal Crash." Available at: https://www.theguardian.com/technology/2024/apr/26/tesla-autopilot-fatal-crash

58. The New York Times (2019). "Apple Card Investigated After Gender

Discrimination Complaints." Available at: https://www.nytimes.com/2019/11/10/business/Apple-credit-card-investigation.html

59. The New York Times (2020). "The Secretive Company That Might End Privacy as We Know It." Available at: https://www.nytimes.com/2020/01/18/technology/clearview-privacy-facial-recognition.html

60. The New York Times (2021). "A.I. Drone May Have Acted on Its Own in Attacking Fighters, U.N. Says." Available at: https://www.nytimes.com/2021/06/03/world/africa/libya-drone.html

61. The New York Times (2023). "Chatbots and Their Alarming Hallucination Rates." Available at: https://www.nytimes.com/2023/11/06/technology/chatbots-hallucination-rates.html

62. The New York Times (2024). "'Deepfake' Caller Poses as Ukrainian Official in Exchange With Key Senator." Available at: https://www.nytimes.com/2024/09/26/us/senator-cardin-deepfake.html

63. The Register (2021). "Facial recog firm Clearview hit with complaints in France, Austria, Italy, Greece and the UK." Available at: https://www.theregister.com/2021/05/27/clearview_europe/

64. The Verge (2018). "Uber halts self-driving tests after pedestrian killed in Arizona." Available at: https://www.theverge.com/2018/3/19/17139518/uber-self-driving-car-fatal-crash-tempe-arizona

65. The Verge (2019). "Apple Card algorithm allegedly discriminates against women, prompting investigation." Available at: https://www.theverge.com/2019/11/11/20958953/apple-credit-card-gender-discrimination-algorithms-black-box-investigation

66. The Wall Street Journal (2015). "Google Mistakenly Tags Black People as 'Gorillas,' Showing Limits of Algorithms." Available at: https://www.wsj.com/articles/BL-DGB-42522

67. The Wall Street Journal (2019). "Fraudsters Used AI to Mimic CEO's Voice in Cybercrime Case." Available at: https://www.wsj.com/articles/fraudsters-use-ai-to-mimic-ceos-voice-in-unusual-cybercrime-case-11567157402

68. United Nations Security Council. (2021). "Final report of the Panel of Experts on Libya established pursuant to Security Council resolution 1973 (2011)." Available at:
https://www.securitycouncilreport.org/atf/cf/%7B65BFCF9B-6D27-4E9C-8CD3-CF6E4FF96FF9%7D/S_2021_229.pdf

69. U.S. Securities and Exchange Commission (2013). "In the Matter of Knight Capital Americas LLC, Administrative Proceeding." Available at:
https://www.sec.gov/files/litigation/admin/2013/34-70694.pdf

70. Williams, B., et al. (2019). "Using AI to Diagnose Patients: Babylon Health." JAMA Network Open. Available at:
https://www.ncbi.nlm.nih.gov/pmc/articles/PMC6532823/#b10

71. Wired (2021). "Zillow's Home-Buying Debacle Shows How Hard It Is to Use AI to Value Real Estate." Available at:
https://www.wired.com/story/zillow-ibuyer-real-estate/

72. Wong A, Otles E, Donnelly JP, Krishnan G, et al. (2021). "External Validation of a Widely Implemented Proprietary Sepsis Prediction Model in Hospitalized Patients." JAMA Internal Medicine. Available at:
https://www.ncbi.nlm.nih.gov/pmc/articles/PMC8218233/

Made in United States
North Haven, CT
04 November 2026

21732948R00088